FOCUS ON

BONNIE AND CLYDE

FILM FOCUS

Ronald Gottesman and Harry M. Geduld
General Editors

THE FILM FOCUS SERIES PRESENTS THE BEST THAT HAS BEEN
WRITTEN ABOUT THE ART OF FILM AND THE MEN WHO CREATED
IT. COMBINING CRITICISM WITH HISTORY, BIOGRAPHY, AND ANAL-
YSIS OF TECHNIQUE, THE VOLUMES IN THE SERIES EXPLORE THE
MANY DIMENSIONS OF THE FILM MEDIUM AND ITS IMPACT ON
MODERN SOCIETY.

JOHN G. CAWELTI, *editor of this volume in the Film Focus
series, is Professor of English and Humanities at the University of Chicago. He is the author of* The Six-Gun Mystique,
*a study of the western novel and film, and of other books and
articles on American cultural history and popular culture.*

FOCUS ON

BONNIE AND CLYDE

◆◇◆

edited by

JOHN G. CAWELTI

73081

A SPECTRUM BOOK

Prentice-Hall, Inc.
Englewood Cliffs, N.J.

Library of Congress Cataloging in Publication Data

CAWELTI, JOHN G   comp.
  Focus on Bonnie and Clyde.

  (Film focus) (A Spectrum Book)
  "Filmography": p. 167.
  Bibliography: p.
  1. Bonnie and Clyde (Motion Picture). I. Title.
PN1997.B6797C3   791.43'7   72–10196
ISBN 0–13–080119–4
ISBN 0–13–080101–1 (pbk)

Printed in the United States of America

10   9   8   7   6   5   4   3   2   1

PRENTICE-HALL INTERNATIONAL, INC. (*London*)
PRENTICE-HALL OF AUSTRALIA, PTY. LTD. (*Sydney*)
PRENTICE-HALL OF CANADA, LTD. (*Toronto*)
PRENTICE-HALL OF INDIA PRIVATE LIMITED (*New Delhi*)
PRENTICE-HALL OF JAPAN, INC. (*Tokyo*)

CONTENTS

ACKNOWLEDGMENTS

Many thanks to Arthur Penn for loaning me his copy of the original script; to Ron Gottesman and Harry and Carolyn Geduld for excellent criticism and extraordinary patience; to David and Leslie Travis for their skillful photographic assistance; to Claudia Wilson for finally getting it all straightened out; to my friends and students for willingly allowing me to plunder their insights about *Bonnie and Clyde*.

And, above all, to Ellen, Jon, Brent, and Andrea Cawelti for letting Bonnie and Clyde usurp so much of my attention, and to Marcia Baker without whose help I could never have managed to finish this anthology.

BONNIE AND CLYDE

Warner Brothers Pictures, 1967, A Tatira-Hiller Production

PRODUCER	Warren Beatty
DIRECTOR	Arthur Penn
SCRIPT	David Newman and Robert Benton
PHOTOGRAPHY	Burnett Guffey, A.S.C.
ART DIRECTOR	Dean Tavoularis
FILM EDITOR	Dede Allen
SOUND	Francis E. Stahl
SET DECORATOR	Raymond Paul
SPECIAL EFFECTS	Danny Lee
COSTUMES	Theodora Van Runkle
SPECIAL CONSULTANT	Robert Towne
MUSIC	Charles Strouse
PRODUCTION MANAGER	Russ Saunders
ASSISTANT TO THE PRODUCER	Elaine Michea
SCRIPT SUPERVISOR	John Dutton
MAKEUP	Robert Jiras
MISS DUNAWAY'S MAKEUP	Warner Brothers Cosmetics
FLATT & SCRUGGS, "FOGGY MOUNTAIN BREAKDOWN"	Courtesy Mercury Records
MEN'S WARDROBE	Andy Matyasi
WOMEN'S WARDROBE	Norma Brown
HAIR STYLIST	Gladys Witten
ASSISTANT DIRECTOR	Jack N. Reddish

CAST

Clyde Barrow	WARREN BEATTY
Bonnie Parker	FAYE DUNAWAY
C. W. Moss	MICHAEL J. POLLARD
Buck Barrow	GENE HACKMAN
Blanche	ESTELLE PARSONS
Frank Hamer	DENVER PYLE
Ivan Moss	DUB TAYLOR
Velma Davis	EVANS EVANS
Eugene Grizzard	GENE WILDER

FOCUS ON

BONNIE AND CLYDE

Introduction:

BONNIE AND CLYDE:
Tradition and Transformation
by JOHN G. CAWELTI

At about 9:15 in the morning of May 23, 1934, near Arcadia, Louisiana, two young desperados from Texas were ambushed and killed by a group of lawmen led by Texas Ranger Frank Hamer. The brief and bloody career of Clyde Barrow and Bonnie Parker, a spree which began in February 1932, had already made the two criminals legendary figures in a period that witnessed the exploits of such public enemies as John Dillinger, Babyface Nelson, Machine-Gun Kelly, and the Barker gang. When their bodies were brought to Arcadia and later to Dallas, thousands of people swarmed around. Souvenir hunters seized bits and pieces of clothing, hair, the death car, and the empty shells left behind the scene of the ambush. The legend of Bonnie and Clyde's life was given a new impetus by the terrible violence of their death. Even today, it is extremely difficult to separate the facts of their careers from the innumerable fantasies that have flourished around them. For some, Bonnie and Clyde came to exemplify the most evil, perverse, and cruel kind of killer. For others, they were modern Robin Hoods, their tragic careers given added poignancy by their love for each other. It is reported that the following inscription is carved on Bonnie's headstone in a Dallas cemetery: "THE LIFE SHE LIVED WILL MAKE THIS WORLD BETTER OFF."

Public fascination with Bonnie and Clyde, and with the other rampaging criminal gangs of the late twenties and early thirties, helped to make the gangster film one of Hollywood's most important

1

and typical creations. Along with the Western, the gangster film, initially defined by Joseph von Sternberg's *Underworld* (1927), Mervyn Le Roy's *Little Caesar* (1931) and William Wellman's *The Public Enemy* (1931), became both a standard Hollywood product and the basis for some of the most powerful and most significant American films. In his study, *The Gangster Film,* John Baxter lists nearly a thousand films in this genre. Not too surprisingly, a number of these films were versions of the story of Bonnie and Clyde, the most important being Fritz Lang's *You Only Live Once* (1937), Nicholas Ray's *They Live by Night* (1948), Joseph H. Lewis's *Gun Crazy* (1949), and William Witney's *The Bonnie Parker Story* (1958).

Not only popular with the American public, the gangster film was an international success. It made a particular impact on the young post-World-War-II French critics and directors who had determined to revitalize the French film: both François Truffaut and Jean-Luc Godard showed their great fascination with the American gangster film in the exciting new film criticism they wrote for journals such as *Cahiers du Cinema.* The content and style of works like Truffaut's *Shoot the Piano Player* and Godard's *Breathless, Band of Outsiders,* and *My Life to Live* reflected the basic influence of the American gangster film on the French New Wave.

Arthur Penn's film, *Bonnie and Clyde,* grew out of this complex cultural and artistic background: the reality and legend of the historical Bonnie and Clyde, the American artistic tradition of the gangster film, and the new-wave French film. The film originally took shape in the minds of two young magazine writers, Robert Benton and David Newman, who, impressed by the new French films, started looking for a subject for a screenplay. Inspiration struck when they read an account of the Barrow gang in John Toland's book, *The Dillinger Days.* Toland's book must have revived Benton's childhood memories of the Bonnie and Clyde legend, for he had grown up in a small Texas town. *Time* reports that the initial Benton-Newman scenario was a frank imitation of Truffaut's striking juxtapositions of comedy and tragedy and that Clyde was characterized as a homosexual who shared a "weird menage à trois" with Bonnie and C. W. Moss. The scenario was offered first to Truffaut and then to Godard, but both directors ultimately turned it down. Interestingly, Godard later made *Pierrot le Fou,* a film greatly resembling the story of Bonnie and Clyde. Finally, the script was purchased by the young actor Warren Beatty, who secured the services of director Arthur Penn. The way the film was shaped under Penn's direction is discussed in my essay, "The Artistic Power of *Bonnie and Clyde*," and can be studied still more completely by using the table of differences (between an earlier version of the script and the final film) on pages 138–45, below.

Bonnie and Clyde was enough of a transformation from the traditional gangster film that when it opened in New York in August 1967, it quickly became a center of critical controversy. Critics such as Bosley Crowther and Page Cook (pp. 22–23 and 23–24, below) responded to the movie with anger and loathing. They felt the film's sympathetic, tragicomic portrayal of a criminal gang represented a kind of artistic immorality that might encourage young people to admire criminals. These critics were distressed, moreover, by the film's historical inaccuracies, its graphic and sensual representation of violence, and its mixture of comedy with violence. Critical disfavor did not prevent audiences from liking the film, however. For some weeks after his scathing review, *New York Times* critic Crowther was bombarded with mail opposing the negative verdict he had rendered on the film. Audiences, particularly young people, mobbed the theaters, making *Bonnie and Clyde* one of the most commercially successful films of 1967. Before long, the public had made *Bonnie and Clyde* into a fad. Double-breasted suits and fedoras of the sort worn by Clyde became a fashion in clothing, while Bonnie's outfits sparked still more frantic maneuvers among those who establish the line and length of women's dresses. Some critics, surprised by the audience acclaim returned to see the film again and wrote new reviews qualifying their earlier, negative verdicts. Finally, when Pauline Kael, the *grande dame* of American film critics, published a long and highly laudatory discussion of the film in *The New Yorker*, the critical verdict had begun to swing into line with the enthusiasm of the public. In the annual competition for various awards, *Bonnie and Clyde* was listed among the Film Daily Critics' Top Ten Pictures of the Year, received a New York Film Critics' award for its script, and two Academy Awards (for cinematography and best supporting actress).

Since its original run, *Bonnie and Clyde* has been revived and is still playing at some commercial theaters. Whether it will turn out to be one of the classic American films remains to be seen, but its impact has already been considerable. Director Arthur Penn went on to make two very different but extremely successful films, *Alice's*

Restaurant and *Little Big Man.* Other filmmakers, such as Roger Corman in *Bloody Mama* and Robert Aldrich in the *Grissom Gang,* have followed Penn's example in their treatments of the gangster theme, though none have achieved the level of artistic success of *Bonnie and Clyde.* Unquestionably, Penn's film heralded, if it did not directly influence, a number of important trends in the films of the late 1960s and early 1970s: the ambiguous mixture of comic and tragic tones, the brutal and shocking depiction of violence, a new openness about problems of sexuality and perversion, a new version of the criminal protagonist, and the quasi-mythical evocation of the epoch of the 1930s. Important new films, such as Hill's *Butch Cassidy and the Sundance Kid,* Peckinpah's *The Wild Bunch* and *Straw Dogs,* Altman's *M*A*S*H* and *McCabe and Mrs. Miller,* and Pollack's *They Shoot Horses, Don't They?,* all show some of these same trends.

Besides a sampling of the initial flurry of positive and negative reviews, this anthology includes many of the useful critical perspectives on *Bonnie and Clyde* that have since appeared. My own essay considers the film as a complex artistic structure, showing how theme, plot, character, and cinematic techniques are welded into a single unified and powerfully moving work. As a foil to this argument for the artistic excellence of the film, Charles Samuels's essay presents the most thorough and most well-supported attack on the film that has yet been mounted. For him, *Bonnie and Clyde's* artistic power is comparable to that of "a bunch of decayed cabbage leaves smeared with catsup."

Both Carolyn Geduld and William J. Free begin their discussions with a consideration of what was for most viewers the most striking aspect of *Bonnie and Clyde:* its combination of contrasting emotional tones, the juxtaposition of delightful, farcical comedy with the most brutal and tragic violence. Geduld sees an important thematic dimension to this contrast: the way these different elements of the film develop the conflict between the gang's tribal or clannish loyalties and the values of society. Free, on the other hand, points out how the movie uses comic devices to engage our sympathies with the characters in order to make our feeling about their destruction more powerful and tragic.

Finally, John Howard Lawson, whose own experience with films goes well back into the thirties, treats *Bonnie and Clyde* as social criticism by comparing it with *The Grapes of Wrath,* John Ford's

major social film of the late thirties. As Lawson points out, the
two films have many things in common, yet *Bonnie and Clyde* embodies a very different kind of social criticism from that of *The
Grapes of Wrath.*

In the remainder of the anthology I have tried to bring together
materials that will help the reader develop a number of different
viewpoints on *Bonnie and Clyde.* Robert Steele raises the moral
issue again in comparing *Bonnie and Clyde* to another contemporary
film about crime, Truman Capote's and Richard Brooks's *In Cold
Blood.* Although I disagree with Steele's critical evaluations, the
general questions he raises about artistic responsibility and cultural
values cannot be avoided in any serious discussion of films dealing,
like *Bonnie and Clyde,* with themes of crime and violence. One important aspect of the question of artistic responsibility is the extent
to which the filmmaker is bound to follow historical fact in his treatment of characters who actually existed. Just how problematic
"historical fact" can be in the case of characters like the real Bonnie
and Clyde can be seen in the conflict of testimony between the historical documents I have included. Although all purport to give
accurate accounts of the death of Bonnie Parker and Clyde Barrow
by persons who were close to the events themselves, there is striking
variation in details.

These various accounts of the real Bonnie and Clyde also shed
light on the film's creation by raising the questions of which historical accounts the film's creators chose to follow and how they
varied these accounts as they scripted and shot the film. Such questions might lead one to look at the film's development through the
changes in various versions of the script. I have included a chart,
giving a systematic description of the differences between an earlier
version of the script and the final film, which should help the reader
see how the structure and intentions of the work were clarified and
certain lines of development intensified. I have also included two
script versions of the crucial love scene in which Bonnie reads her
poem to Clyde. Though one of these versions is the final script,
Penn made further changes in the process of shooting and final editing which can be seen in the film itself. I hope that these materials,
together with the content outline of the film, will aid readers in
appreciating the rich and complex structure of *Bonnie and Clyde.*

The editor of a volume of essays on a work of art that is barely
half a decade old must view the future of his judgments with a cer-

tain degree of trepidation and uncertainty. To assert that so new a film is worth the serious and permanent attention of future audiences is something of a gamble. Yet I have found that repeated viewings and careful analytical consideration of *Bonnie and Clyde* have borne out my initial feeling about the film's special artistic merits, and I hope that this volume of essays will contribute to the continuing exploration of this remarkable creative achievement.

Arthur Penn
by JIM HILLIER

While as a rule we should trust the tale, not the artist, Penn is among the most articulate of film-makers, acutely conscious of his artistic and social preoccupations. This account of Penn's life and collation of his statements from interviews aims not to explain the films but rather to set them in context.

Penn was born in 1922. After his parents divorced he spent his school years between his mother and brother in New York and New Hampshire and his father in Philadelphia. He began to study watchmaking, his father's trade, but in 1943 enlisted in the Army. During Army training he started a small theatre group, where he first associated with Fred Coe. Towards the end of the war Penn voluntarily lost rank to join Joshua Logan's military theatre company. On demobilization in 1946, he continued his studies, first in North Carolina, then in Perugia and Florence.

Penn had studied literature and thought first of becoming a writer, then of working in the theatre. But 1951 saw him starting a career in television, where he worked almost consistently till his movie début in 1957. By 1952 Penn had graduated to co-director of the Colgate Comedy Hour where he worked at one time with Jerry Lewis, said to be at the origins of *Mickey One*. From 1953 Penn was directing drama programmes, with Fred Coe as producer. Penn says, "at that time TV was poor, so we were free." [1] It was an auspicious time to be working in television. Penn was one of a group of young directors which included Lumet, Frankenheimer and Mulligan. He worked with writers like Chayevsky, William Gibson,

From Screen *10, no. 1 (January–February 1969): 5–12. Reprinted by permission of* Screen.

[1] *Télérama*, October 6, 1963.

Horton Foote, Leslie Stevens, and actors like Kim Stanley, E. G. Marshall, Paul Newman, some of whom were later involved in his films.

Penn had already directed *Blue Denim* on stage in 1954 and after *The Left-Handed Gun* in 1957 he turned almost completely to Broadway theatre. There he directed people like Henry Fonda, Anne Bancroft, Patty Duke in plays by William Gibson (*Two for the Seesaw, The Miracle Worker*) and Lillian Hellman (*Toys in the Attic*). Though he has never again worked so intensely in it as during the five-year gap between his first and second films, Penn has maintained contact with the theatre.

Penn's TV and theatre experience has obviously influenced his film career, not least in terms of the writers and actors with whom he worked. Fred Coe gave Penn his first chance in the cinema and may well have been decisive in ensuring that Penn continued to make films after *The Left-Handed Gun*. Penn has always refused to be put under contract, thus preserving the freedom he enjoyed in TV and theatre. It was in TV that Penn first used several cameras simultaneously. "I think the system is excellent because it allows you not to break the continuity of acting." [2] As one might expect from a theatre director and habitué of Actors' Studio, actors are important to Penn. He considers Kazan the greatest director of actors and has followed his method, which Penn describes as "half improvisation, and half control." "I prefer to choose actors from theatre and, what is more, from Actors' Studio, because I like to leave actors a certain freedom and Actors' Studio people often have marvellous ideas." [3]

The Left-Handed Gun, Penn's first film, was made in Hollywood in low-budget conditions. He says he virtually lost control of the film and has described the experience as unpleasant, but his feelings seem to have been strongly influenced by the film's reception. "In America, nobody devoted more than three lines to the film and nobody went to see it. It was then that I thought I could no longer work in Hollywood, that I couldn't stick it any longer. So I went back to New York and my theatre work. . . ." [4] Even at this time, Penn felt Hollywood was dying, partly due to the McCarthyist scare: "The big companies got scared, made crazy films, losing all contact

[2] Ibid.
[3] *Cinémonde,* September 21, 1965.
[4] *Cahiers du Cinéma* 140 (February 1963).

with real life, with the people. Indirectly this was the death of the big studio. That's why we're now witnessing a more intimate cinema, a freer cinema perhaps." [5]

Penn's dejection after *The Left-Handed Gun* seems to have gone further than mere disenchantment with Hollywood. "I was so disappointed by the American cinema that I didn't think I would make other films. But a friend (Coe) asked me to shoot *The Miracle Worker*. It was a quite different experience since we did the shooting in New York." [6] But by this time, something else had happened: *The Left-Handed Gun* had been shown in Europe. "I only really regained confidence in myself when I read the critical reviews published in the French press. They had seen it and understood it. It was a miracle." [7]

In contrast to *The Left-Handed Gun,* Penn was intimately involved at every stage of *The Miracle Worker.* He was pleased with the experience, although he felt it was a "too literal and too talkative" translation from play to film, and found some scenes "very theatrical" in effect. These feelings may have induced Penn to be very consciously "cinematic" in *Mickey One.* Despite the unhappy interlude on *The Train* in 1963, when Penn was replaced by Frankenheimer, at Burt Lancaster's request but without explanation, *The Miracle Worker*'s success in America helped to enable Penn to make *Mickey One* on the East Coast again and in conditions of almost absolute freedom. But he recognized that freedom also had its problems. "I am free but it can be terrifying. It really is easier now to get authorization to deal with various subjects. What is more difficult is to know the truth about those subjects." [8]

After *Mickey One,* Penn said that "it ought to have been a better film, for I had the most total freedom." [9] Perhaps this thought softened his attitude to the Hollywood "machine." He recognized, probably under the influence of the French critics who praised his work, that "the American cinema is a technically exquisite, immaculate machine which in the hands of a few masters like Hitchcock and Hawks has become an Art. But I doubt very much that this cinema is capable also of giving essentially modern works, delicately moving,

[5] Ibid.
[6] *Cinéma 68,* no. 125 (April 1968).
[7] *Télérama,* October 6, 1963.
[8] *Cahiers du Cinéma* 150–51 (December 1963–January 1964).
[9] *Cahiers du Cinéma* 196 (December 1967).

personal works." [7] Penn admits to being influenced by Godard and
Truffaut—"with them, you can no longer make films as you made
them before." [4] What, for Penn, militates against personal expression in Hollywood is the system of working "by committee." He
regarded *The Chase* as "the chance to work on a grand scale . . . I
had already worked in Hollywood and it wasn't very pleasant.
Today, I'm trying to find out if I was wrong seven years ago, and if
I can now master the big machine." [10] "It's a dreadful thing to
make a film with so many technicians around you, so many very
qualified, very clever people. . . . Each person surrounding you
knows exactly how your idea should be realized and what emerges
finally . . . is not your idea, but the archetype of the Hollywood
idea, the commonplace, the banal. If you want to avoid that, you
must constantly say no to your collaborators: systematically refuse
their proposals, from a nuance of colour to the choice of a tie,
you've got to change everything! . . . Very quickly, you no longer
have either enough interest or energy to be able to do everything
yourself, and that's why, finally, *The Chase* became a Hollywood
film rather than a Penn film." [11]

Penn values artistic freedom too highly to see the lesson of
Mickey One, that total freedom may not suit him, and that the tensions involved in working with "the machine" may emerge as a
creative tension. Certainly, Penn's most striking films are those
where he is working within the system, within narrative conventions
and within a formula or genre. Working this way seems to make him
work against the conventions, both technically and thematically, and
destroy our expectations of the genre by, for example, pushing the
violence commonplace in westerns, or gangster films, to extremes of
physicality. *Mickey One,* which despite its American preoccupations,
is in its abstraction more like a European film, may hint at the
dangers inherent in Penn consciously rejecting American cinematic
traditions.

Despite his problems with the "system," Penn has become progressively more interested in cinema and less in theatre. Broadway, and
even off-Broadway, has become conventional and its audience
"limited," bourgeois, white, self-satisfied. . . ." [12] "The supposedly
serious theatre attacks none of the fundamental values of its public.

[10] *Cahiers du Cinéma* 171 (October 1965).
[11] *Cahiers du Cinéma* 150–51 (December 1963–January 1964).
[12] Ibid.

The cinema does: its effect is made at a very personal level, like a book or a poem." [13] "There was a time when, if you were working in theatre as a "serious" artist and went off to Hollywood, you were prostituting yourself, but now it's the opposite." [14] But then Hollywood has also changed: "The men who direct the studios are young . . . that makes a big difference. It was very difficult before, when there were those old kings, to talk to them about modern life. They didn't know what it was. Their values were from another time, excessively moralizing. . . . Hollywood studios are now only places where you get technical equipment . . . Hollywood as a 'place' no longer exists." [15]

"All my life I've never known any moment when we had ceased making war. The gangsters were all-powerful when I was young; I went to war at eighteen years of age, then there was Korea, and now Vietnam." [16] Penn sees violence as "a part of the character of America. It began with the western, the "frontier." America is a country where people realize their ideas in violent ways—we have no tradition of persuasion, idealism or legality . . . Kennedy was slaughtered. We are in Vietnam killing people and getting ourselves killed. We're living in a society of violence . . . I find myself forced to explain it, to be concerned with it. . . . What I wanted to say in *Mickey One*, for example, was that we are living in an age of violence—we undergo a sort of contract with violence during our own lives." [17]

Penn's films, whether set in the past or not, are concerned with American violence and morality now. In *Bonnie and Clyde* "we wanted to make a modern film whose action takes place in the past." [18] Speaking in December 1967 of his next project, Penn described it as "concerning what was really the fate of the Red Indian at the time of Custer. Obviously, the analogy with the Negroes is great. But, at the moment, I wouldn't know how to make a film about Negroes. It would be limited, partial or romanticized." [19] His new film would be "fiction, not a documentary: in an adventure

---

[13] *Positif* 89 (November 1967).
[14] *Cahiers du Cinéma* 196 (December 1967).
[15] *Cinéma 68*, no. 125 (April 1968).
[16] *Positif* 89 (November 1967).
[17] Ibid.
[18] *Cinéma 68*, no. 125 (April 1968).
[19] *Cahiers du Cinéma* 196 (December 1967).

story you can underline political problems in a didactic way." [20] "I work on certain things which concern me, things I cannot see otherwise than in relation to the social and political role of the United States in the world. I work on facts relative to the problems raised by the role of leader that this country has been forced to play, its lack of preparation for that role, and the disparity between the level of thought in the United States and elsewhere." [21]

When we see, in Penn's work, the capacity for violence in characters almost totally unable to cope with it emotionally and morally, unable to comprehend the implications of their actions, we can see this as in some ways analogous to America's world role—wielding immense power without recognizing its full implications. In *Bonnie and Clyde* Penn says he tried to describe the social morality prevalent in the South—"very moralizing, very puritanical, but integrating indissolubly into itself a form of violence against other human beings which, seen from outside, seems absolutely intolerable," a gulf between "private rigour and public violence." [22]

This helps to explain the power of myth in America and hence its presence in Penn's films. The adoption of heroes and myth provides, in part, a focal point, a sublimation of "public violence." "The idea of what happened behind legends has always interested me." [23] By exposing a reality, not necessarily a documentary one, behind myth, Penn removes the prop which myth provides. All his films use myth in some form. Billy the Kid and Bonnie and Clyde are established folk legends, and there is a clear line between them—"in the mythology of the American West, the automobile replaced the horse as the symbol of the outlaw." [24] His intention in *The Left-Handed Gun* was "to find, through the Billy the Kid myth, which is very alive in the United States, the deep myths of Greek tragedy. *The Left-Handed Gun* is Oedipus in the West. There are in the western conventions a ritual, a mythic simplicity, which make it a marvellous tragic mould." [25] In the film, Moultrie provokes Billy's death when he discovers Billy does not live up to the heroic image Moultrie has created in his stories. In *Bonnie and Clyde*, Penn

[20] *Cinéma 68*, no. 125 (April 1968).
[21] *Cahiers du Cinéma* 171 (October 1965).
[22] *Positif* 89 (November 1967).
[23] *Cinéma 68*, no. 125 (April 1968).
[24] *Positif* 89 (November 1967).
[25] *Télérama*, October 6, 1963.

justifies the historical inaccuracies and beautiful people by stressing that "we were dealing with the mythic aspects of their lives." [26] The whole structure of the film, the banjo ballad (recalling folk ballads like Woody Guthrie's about Pretty Boy Floyd), is like elements of myth—the exhilaration of the chases—punctuated by sequences of violent reality, with the music faltering when Bonnie and Clyde are so wounded as to exclude the possibility of romantic myth. There are elements of similar banjo strains accompanying Bubber at the start of *The Chase*, which traces the elevation, by the community, of Bubber Reeves into a hero, a mythic figure. *Mickey One* can be seen as Modern Man, a hero of our times. In *The Miracle Worker*, "there too there is a myth at the origin. All American schoolchildren have heard about Helen Keller." [27] Penn's film exposes the violent effort behind the simple, noble legend. And myth need not be confined to characters—Penn has also been concerned, for example, with "the myth of easy death." [28]

The endings of Penn's films tend to sustain myth. Penn's own original ending to *The Left-Handed Gun*, a village procession with Billy's body, was a "little ritual to close the cycle of the legend." [29] After the bloody deaths in *Bonnie and Clyde*, Penn is conscious of endowing the final deaths with a mythic dimension by giving them "a more 'abstract,' less physical character." [30] The shooting down of Bubber Reeves in *The Chase* (part of Penn's addition to the script) secures his heroic stature in the community. The end of *The Miracle Worker* has, in contrast to most of the film, the nobility and exhilaration normally associated with the Keller myth. But Penn likes also to inject a disturbing note of actuality. Most notably, Bubber is shot down "à la Kennedy," as Penn says, but he also remarked that in Clyde's death "there's even a bit of Warren's head which jumps, like Kennedy's in that famous photograph of his death." [31]

Penn's sustenance of myth works ultimately as an indictment of the society which creates it. His heroes tend to have potential for spontaneity, open acceptance of life, but this potential is lost in

---

[26] *New York Times*, September 17, 1967.
[27] *Télérama*, October 6, 1963.
[28] *Cahiers du Cinéma* 140 (February 1963).
[29] *Cahiers du Cinéma* 196 (December 1967).
[30] Ibid.
[31] Ibid.

the auto-destructive urges of the heroes and the destructive forces at work in the society from which they come. Their potential and their lack of awareness of the social implications of their acts stem from the same source, the characters' child-like quality. Penn acknowledges his closeness to the world of childhood, something he recognizes and admires in Truffaut—"that comes from my own existence. When I was three, my parents divorced and I stopped believing in the adult world." [32] Certainly, "family" problems disturb Penn's characters. Billy the Kid kills when Tunstall, his "father," is murdered, and reaches out hopelessly for a "family" in Celsa and Saval. Annie Sullivan and the Kellers battle over who should be Helen's "family." Bubber Reeves rejects his parents and Jake Rogers seeks in Bubber and Anna an alternative "family." When Bonnie fails to communicate with her mother, Clyde tells her "I'm your family now."

Penn greatly admires Ford and Kazan, both of whose films have intense involvement with the growth and problems of American society. Like Kazan, Penn sees his characters' actions as determined by their social environment. What interested him in *The Chase* was "not so much the hero but the framework in which he evolves, the society which transforms him." [33] Similarly, Penn's only serious additions to the script of *Bonnie and Clyde* concerned the dramatization of the era, in sequences like the old farmer turned off his land and the Okie camp (acknowledged by Penn as "a sort of homage" to Ford's *The Grapes of Wrath*). "When Bonnie and Clyde were killed, they were regarded as enormous folk heroes by many people. To dismiss them simply as killers, or pariahs, would be inaccurate. Because they were folk heroes, it's necessary to examine the times to see *why* they should be folk heroes. The times were out of joint . . . A time creates its own myths and heroes. If the heroes are less than admirable, that is a clue to the times." [34]

[32] *Cahiers du Cinéma* 171 (October 1965).
[33] *Cinémonde*, September 21, 1965.
[34] *New York Times*, September 17, 1967.

BONNIE AND CLYDE:
An Interview with Arthur Penn
by JEAN-LOUIS COMOLLI and ANDRÉ S. LABARTHE

In Bonnie and Clyde *you carry to the extreme a tendency to juxtapose sequences which explore the violence of various situations to their fullest* . . .

I wanted the film to have a certain rhythm, a nervous montage. Also, my memory of Bonnie and Clyde was from snapshots; I didn't want a moving camera that would stay on a scene for a long time. I wanted something more kaleidoscopic.

Each shot in your film seems to serve a dual purpose: it carries forward the film's story and it also adds a new piece of information to what went on before, with a technique which makes each sequence almost autonomous . . .

It is in the service of the notion of irony. Very often we would lead the audience to believe one thing, and then in the next sequence we turn around. For example, in the beginning of the film, at the abandoned farm, when the farmer says that the bank took his house away: at that point Bonnie and Clyde know they're robbers, but they don't know what they want to rob. They know that they're outlaws, but for what? At the end of that sequence we have a close-up of Warren saying, "We rob banks." It's an afterthought; he discovers afterward what he was doing earlier. We are dealing with a sort of primitive intellect. Clyde is not a very intelligent or complicated man, but a man full of desire to act. He must act but he doesn't know why. In this film, that was what we meant by "doing." Socially, the people were paralyzed by the Depression, for example,

From Evergreen Review *12, no. 55 (June 1968): 61–63. Reprinted by permission of Éditions de L'Étoile and Grove Press, Inc.*

the scene in the camp near the end is nearly stylized in its im-
mobility. I was trying to say that everybody else was still—frozen
by the atmosphere, by the Depression. At least Bonnie and Clyde
were mobile and functioning—sometimes in behalf of foolish things,
sometimes self-destructively—but at least they functioned.

*Just when Clyde dies there's a shot from above—he turns, we see
him from behind, his body rises like a wave, and then the shot
changes. Was that a preconceived idea or did you get it as you were
shooting?*

I had the idea before I started shooting. I wanted to get the spasm
of death, and so I used four cameras, each one at a different speed,
24, 48, 72, and 96, I think, and different lenses, so that I could cut
to get the shock and at the same time the ballet of death. There's a
moment in death when the body no longer functions, when it becomes an object and has a certain kind of detached ugly beauty. It
was that aspect that I was trying to get.

What about Bonnie's death?

Bonnie was trapped in the car and I wanted the two kinds of
death: Clyde's to be rather like a ballet, and Bonnie's to have the
physical shock. So we shot it with all those different cameras. We
put on the bullet holes—and there's even a piece of Warren's head
that comes off, like that famous photograph of Kennedy.

What did you ask the actress to do at that point?

Just to be, simply to enact the death, to fall and follow the
laws of gravity. Faye was trapped behind the wheel. We tied one
leg to the gear shift so that she would feel free to fall, but wouldn't
fall out of the car. We shot it three or four times to get this feeling,
and changed speed and lenses constantly to get this sort of change
of pace in space and time.

And this also creates an aura of unreality about Clyde's death . . .

Yes, because I knew it would be the end of the film. We could
have done a killing which would be very gross and vulgar—really
obscene and terribly ugly—where you see him simply torn apart, but
that didn't seem to me to be an accurate end, because the death of
these two people is a foregone conclusion. It's not as if it just
happened. Since you know it's going to happen, I figure you should
do an abstraction of it rather than a replica of it.

Wouldn't it have been preferable to end Bonnie and Clyde *with
the shot of Beatty turning, rather than shots of the town hall with
the people arriving?*

We tried that and it seemed too abrupt, and because it was so abrupt it became almost self-conscious. It gave me the feeling of not having those last few notes in a symphony. You know that this is the end but you need the last three or four notes just to finish it, for form only, because it's over as far as content. The moment he rolls over, the moment her hand stops, that was the end of the story. To end there seemed to change the meaning, to take away from its faintly abstract quality. It seemed like we were trying to do a replica, brutal and severe; we wanted a mythical, legendary, balletic ending.

Did you ever conceive of the construction of your film in terms of one or more musical forms?

The two young journalists who wrote the script had interviewed Flatt and Scruggs in Nashville, Tennessee, and suggested we use the five-string country banjo. That gave us an idea of what kind of music to use. We used Flatt and Scruggs and a young composer who wrote some other music in the same spirit.

In the beginning of Bonnie and Clyde *the tone is one of burlesque and then becomes pathetic. Did this shift exist in the scenario itself?*

Sometimes that happens but ordinarily it's not conscious. It started as a chronicle of some amusing kids who dug up these funny things to do—a little bit outside the law but not too serious. The way we set up the first killing—they can't get the car out, the man jumps on the running board of the car, and they shoot him right in the face—it's to come right out of laughter. The idea was for us to be laughing and suddenly it was just to happen—"I killed somebody, I didn't mean to do that, I was just robbing a bank, I didn't . . ."—it was to have that kind of innocence.

All deaths are extremely distressing and very bloody . . .

Very bloody and very painful. My own experience—it's not very broad—is that blood always surprises me, the amount of blood—too much. It recalls Shakespeare's line, "Who would have thought the old man could have had so much blood in him?" In film, when you show a death, it should have that shock effect. But at the end of *Bonnie and Clyde,* we didn't do the same kind of death; we were trying to change the character of death, to make their deaths more legendary than real.

Is it in order to arouse conflicting feelings in the public that you utilize these constant shifts in tone?

In *Bonnie and Clyde,* we don't have a story of very strong characters. They're relatively shallow, rather empty people as far as we know. Nice enough, and with certain problems, but we don't have a moral dilemma which would help us to understand what the characters are going through in their interior lives. Consequently, we had to deal more at the level of the outer side, like the cartoon, more the outline. I though in terms of cartoons—each frame changing. Here we laugh, here we cry, here we laugh again, and so we cut the film like that and the images were made up like that instead of long, fluid ones.

Which gives Bonnie and Clyde *a playful dimension. But doesn't it seem dangerous to you to be able to manipulate at will the reactions of the public which, being less interested in the characters, is only responsive to your manipulation?*

Yes, it seems to me a little dangerous, but it seemed to be the best way to tell this story. We have to begin with the fact that these two people were killers; they were gangsters; they seemed to have almost no conscience. Since I couldn't find a deep interior life for them, I decided to really stay outside, to change as swiftly as I could from one sentiment to another. I hope that a certain kind of life comes out of that but, in point of fact, you know very little of what they really were feeling or thinking because it's more of a chronicle than the story of any one person's struggle with his time. We used laughter to get the audience to feel like a member of the gang, to have the feeling of adventure, a feeling of playing together. Then, near the end of the film, we begin to turn a little bit. The humor fades when Bonnie says she wants to see her mother. When the mother says to her, "Don't live three miles from me because you'll be dead if you do," the humor in the film really ends. We hope by then that you're already trapped, that you're caught in the film as a member of the gang and now you have to go along. Bonnie's and Clyde's deaths really begin at that point and from there on it's waiting out history.

What are your plans for future films?

I'm working on one about an American Indian. Again it's a comic story, but we'll have scenes that will be as terrible as the lot of the American Indian really is—and really was in Custer's time. Of course, the analogy is to the American Negro, but at the moment at least, I don't know how to do a film about the American Negro that wouldn't be a distortion or a romance, or too limited in its views.

Can you explain to us the kind of problems you would encounter in making a film about Negroes?

I have to have perspective. I don't have a view sufficiently complete to be able to know how to make a film about it. I can tell lots of incidents that would be terrible and unpleasant and show injustice, but they wouldn't be saying anything because I don't know the end. Making a film about the Indians might help me to understand that.

It's very interesting that during a screening of *Bonnie and Clyde* one evening, five Negroes present there completely identified with Bonnie and Clyde. They were delighted. They said: "This is the way; that's the way to go, baby. Those cats were all right." They really understood, because in a certain sense the American Negro has the same kind of attitude of "I have nothing more to lose" that was true during the Depression for Bonnie and Clyde. It is true now of the American Negro. He is really at the point of revolution—it's rebellion, not riot.

REVIEWS

BOSLEY CROWTHER

❖❖❖

A raw and unmitigated campaign of sheer press-agentry has been trying to put across the notion that Warner Brothers' "Bonnie and Clyde" is a faithful representation of the desperado careers of Clyde Barrow and Bonnie Parker, a notorious team of bank robbers and killers who roamed Texas and Oklahoma in the post-Depression years.

It is nothing of the sort. It is a cheap piece of bald-faced slap-stick comedy that treats the hideous depredations of that sleazy, moronic pair as though they were as full of fun and frolic as the jazz-age cut-ups in "Thoroughly Modern Millie." And it puts forth Warren Beatty and Faye Dunaway in the leading roles, and Michael J. Pollard as their sidekick, a simpering, nose-picking rube, as though they were striving mightily to be the Beverly Hillbillies of next year.

It has Mr. Beatty clowning broadly as the killer who fondles various types of guns with as much nonchalance and dispassion as he airily twirls a big cigar, and it has Miss Dunaway squirming grossly as his thrill-seeking, sex-starved moll. It is loaded with farcical hold-ups, screaming chases in stolen getaway cars that have the antique appearance and speeded-up movement of the clumsy vehicles of the Keystone Cops, and indications of the impotence of Barrow, until Bonnie writes a poem about him to extol his prowess, that are as ludicrous as they are crude.

Such ridiculous, camp-tinctured travesties of the kind of people these desperados were and of the way people lived in the dusty Southwest back in those barren years might be passed off as candidly commercial movie comedy, nothing more, if the film weren't red-dened with blotches of violence of the most grisly sort.

Arthur Penn, the aggressive director, has evidently gone out of his way to splash the comedy holdups with smears of vivid blood as as-

From The New York Times, *August 14, 1967.* © *1967 by The New York Times Company. Reprinted by permission.*

tonished people are machine-gunned. And he has staged the terminal scene of the ambuscading and killing of Barrow and Bonnie by a posse of policemen with as much noise and gore as is in the climax of "The St. Valentine's Day Massacre."

This blending of farce with brutal killings is as pointless as it is lacking in taste, since it makes no valid commentary upon the already travestied truth. And it leaves an astonished critic wondering just what purpose Mr. Penn and Mr. Beatty think they serve with this strangely antique, sentimental claptrap, which opened yesterday at the Forum and the Murray Hill.

This is the film that opened the Montreal International Festival!

PAGE COOK

◈◈

Bonnie and Clyde is so incompetently written, acted, directed and produced it would not be worth noticing were a claque not attempting to promote the idea that its sociopathology is art. The claque even succeeded in having *Bonnie and Clyde* be the opening night picture at Montreal's recent International Film Festival.

The script of *Bonnie and Clyde,* by David Newman and Robert Benton, is dementia praecox of the most pointless sort. That is, it endeavors to do simultaneously such antithetical things as: 1) "explain" the Barrow gang of real-life punks who killed 18 people in the course of Texas-Oklahoma hold-ups in the Depression days of the '30s; 2) *kid* these real-life hold-ups and murders via slap-stick (very amateurishly); 3) deploy male impotence (Clyde's) throughout the film as *an aphrodisiac for pathics of both sexes;* 4) wallow in sadomasochism (the camera dwells on an eye as it is shot from its socket, on a head that is blown apart); 5) arouse sympathy for Clyde Barrow and Bonnie Parker when the police ultimately ambush them and gun them down.

From Films in Review *18, no. 8 (October 1967): 504–5. Reprinted by permission of* Films in Review.

Who is the producer of so adolescently ignorant a film? Warren Beatty, who also plays Clyde, and, in doing so, adds his own ignorances to the character-inconsistencies of the script. Who directed? Arthur Penn, whose artistic integrity is about on the level of Beatty's acting ability—i.e., close to zero. I regret to say so competent a craftsman as Burnett Guffey consented to color-photograph this degenerate farrago. But I do not regret to say Charles Strouse "composed" the music. That he would be willing to provide smarty-pant, Keystone Kop guitar tinkles by Flatt and Scruggs for this film's chase sequences, will long be the index of *his* artistic integrity.

I *am* sorry to say Faye Dunaway and Michael J. Pollard are in the cast. The latter has a small acting range, but is often creative within its limits (wholly physical). Association with *dreck* like *Bonnie and Clyde* can do him professional harm. It can do even greater harm to Miss Dunaway, who has acting ability as well as looks.

One final word: there is *evil* in the *tone* of the writing, acting and direction of this film, the calculated effect of which is to incite in the young the delusion that armed robbery and murder are mere "happenings."

RICHARD SCHICKEL

◆◇◆

Controversy picks the strangest places to settle down and make trouble. Take a stylish but seriously flawed movie called *Bonnie and Clyde* which has split the movie critics and serious viewers right down the middle. As you probably know by now, it is a heavily fictionalized recounting of the gaudy rise and speedy demise of Bonnie Parker and Clyde Barrow, small-time bank robbers who terrorized and titillated the dust-bowl country for several years during the Great Depression. The film tries to transcend the customs

From Life Magazine *63 (October 13, 1967): 16. Reprinted by permission of the author.*

of the gangster genre. Despite its faults, it is worth the serious viewer's attention.

What it is not worthy of is either the terribly intense praise or the equally strident damnation that have been visited upon it by critics and audiences. One reviewer, in an almost unprecedented display of overkill, issued three separate and distinct attacks—for historical inaccuracy, excessive violence, moral turpitude and, I guess, bad breath. He was instantly answered by colleagues and readers in terms as outraged as if he had failed to respond to some latter-day Sistine Chapel. I invite all men of goodwill to join me here on the nice, soft grass of the middle ground.

There is much *Bonnie and Clyde* which one can praise highly. Director Arthur Penn has caught, without seeming to strain, the aridity and emptiness of the countryside through which Bonnie, Clyde and the rest of their addled mob rattled at dangerous speeds in a succession of stolen, comically antique cars to pull their undistinguished jobs, and in the process he has created an arresting visual equivalent of their blank, bleak inner lives. The script by Robert Benton and David Newman emphasizes to good effect that the robbers were at least as interested in their press clippings as they were in money. Everyone concerned keeps the violence which attended their activities casual, mindless, childlike. This has disconcerted many observers, but I think it is esthetically correct, for it carries none of the sado-sexual overtones common in today's representations of violence.

What emerges from these good aspects of the film is a comment on the quality of some American lives. Bonnie and Clyde are the products of the rootlessness of ill-taught youth growing up absurd in a period of historical transition. The parallel between the middle 1930s and the middle 1960s is never too far from the minds of the movie's creators. By stressing the ordinariness of the landscape and society that nurtured these thrill seekers, by making them comical rubes instead of glamorous jet-setters, the film's makers manage to hit us more stingingly where we live than others who have tried to signal the same familiar message.

Why, then, the vague feeling of dissatisfaction which the film leaves? Partly it is the thumping emphasis on period costume, decor and music. It is all awfully cute and surely enhances the movie's appeal as idle entertainment. But it dulls its cutting edge; what might have been a savage purging satire on an American watershed, an important starting point for much of what we now call "modern," often degenerates into an arch attempt to get us to giggle along with the gang.

Then there is the acting. There are three marvelous supporting performances, by baby-fat Michael J. Pollard as the simpleton driver-mechanic, by Gene Hackman as Clyde's heartily all-American brother and by Estelle Parsons as his hysterically blithering bride. They are gifted actors whose energy and imagination simply compel the suspension of disbelief. The trouble arises in the title roles, essayed by Faye Dunaway and Warren Beatty. An A for effort—they seem honestly to be trying to give us that combination of basic moronism and class ignorance that created the vicious vacuity of the real Bonnie and Clyde. But, alas, they remain movie stars. Try as they will, they seem at all times to be just kidding, folks. Underneath these funny make-ups and mannerisms are the intelligent, glamorous people you all know and love. At its very heart, at the very place where it must be strongest, *Bonnie and Clyde* is at its weakest and least authentic.

In the last analysis, then, the film fails not for lack of good—if hardly original or brilliant—intentions, but because those who carried the greatest weight of responsibility for it lacked the will and the nerve to follow their instincts and their intentions the final few steps of the way to fulfillment. What might have been a break-through for the American screen falls back in confusion at the final barriers to self-realization.

PETER COLLIER

❖◈◈◈❖

Bonnie Parker and Clyde Barrow, those shabby neurotics dangling ghostly in the limbo of America's undigested and possibly indigestible past, have had their second coming this past movie

From Ramparts *6, no. 16 (May 1968): 16–22.* © *Ramparts Magazine, Incorporated, 1968. Reprinted by permission of the author.*

season. As it turned out, their return was more miraculous than any-one could have foreseen, far more than even their original death, which was front page news in the New York Times. It has been nothing short of apocalyptic, and the two of them have been re-warded with the highest honor America's pop culture is capable of bestowing: enshrinement as a cult with a genuine cultic following.

As such things usually are, their rebirth was perfectly timely, in-volving the intersection of their potential with our needs. Perhaps the message is that at this point in time, we deserve each other. Those who were delighted by David Levine's cartoon in the New York Review of Books depicting LBJ, his face cagey with corruption, as Clyde and Dean Rusk as his simpering, liver-spotted Bonnie, prob-ably saw it as the perfect comment on these two international criminals. It is—but they also comment on Bonnie and Clyde. Symbols and symbolized: they are all of a kind.

But this is just a fairly delicate nuance, especially in the face of a phenomenon which is picking up speed as quickly as the Barrow Gang. Clearly, they have taken the country by storm once again, picking up mass-cult converts and fellow-travelers as they go, and driving the arbiters of Official Culture like Time magazine into re-peated frenzies of exegesis and explanation, each less literate than the last. Bonnie and Clyde are a happening, both for us and of us, and perfect in their dimensions. They are, in fact, reminiscent of another happening from a far-off time—the resurrection of the morally stale Davy Crockett in the '50s.

Walt Disney, whose tolerance for ambiguity was never high, took Crockett, a buffoonish coonskin demagogue with what seems to have been dangerously spastic politics, and transformed him into a popu-list hero who was quite certain of his own inner light and able to reduce the thorniest problem to a simple folk formula. Crockett be-came the rugged individualist, that most abused of all American ideals, the one most often invoked when the lid is on.

Disney's Cold War mini-epic bowdlerized Crockett's character and rewrote a small amount of history. Moreover, the Crockett myth contained those dangerous oversimplifications by which America has always avoided facing up to complex and demanding experi-ences.

But Davy Crockett wasn't the first of his kind and Bonnie and Clyde won't be the last, although they may wind up as the most suc-cessful. The second coming of heroes is a conventional gambit in America's fantasies about itself—a gambit which, in our time, has idealized and romanticized an earlier historical time when things are seen as having been easier and better. We have not used the past for the potential instruction it contains, but as a defense mechanism to help us avoid responding realistically to the present. The past becomes either a whipping post—the function of Munich, say, for those who want to obliterate the "yellow peril"—or a storehouse from which we dredge up those characters who provide a fantasy framework for our own times.

Whatever else it is, *Bonnie and Clyde* is not a gangster movie. That film genre has seen its day; the attempts to revive it always seem either like Time-Life "documentaries" on the Mafia or a recast of "The Untouchables." Unlike John Dillinger, say, the Barrow Gang didn't have an urban base of operations. They ranged far and wide over the middle of this country, from Iowa to Texas. They belong with Davy Crockett and the other more or less frontier characters who reappear periodically to prop up the moral superstructure of the myth of the West.

Billy the Kid, seen up close in his own time as a reflex killer with mongoloid features and mentality; Wyatt Earp, pimp and feudist; Bill Hickok, a smalltime lawman for whom the back was such a natural target that he usually took great pains not to expose his own —they and many others like them are the stuff on which America's wet dreams about its own moral fiber are based. And all of them return periodically in the mass media as guardians of the notion— probably more American than Maoist—that morality begins down the barrel of a gun, even though the finger on the trigger may be idealistically reluctant.

Bonnie and Clyde, at least in Arthur Penn's nicely made movie, are different, of course, mainly because nobody bothered to force them into the mold of inarticulate protectors of some kind of necessary order—the usual role for the resurrected Western hero. But still, in their brief, flashy cinematic life, they do have a kind of romantic quality—as a machine-gunning, hot-rodding Robin Hood and Maid Marian exuding a spicy aroma of appealing contemporary sexual confusion. They have their wicked Sheriff of Nottingham in Frank Hamer Sr., the Texas Ranger who took a leave of absence from his regular duties to track them down and oversee their execution—and who, in the logic of the film, is the representative of a corrupt law and order: the beautiful people are doubtless his victims (and it is a short step for a viewer of the right age and politics to add, "just like the rest of us").

Bonnie and Clyde have been dealt a greasy deck of cards and are playing the best game they can. But they deny the law without affirming a higher one. Their celluloid lives make no real criticism of the status quo that supposedly oppresses them. It is a myth of pop nihilism; it is Andy Warhol's serial put-ons packaged in a dramatic context with all of Hollywood's savvy behind it.

Bonnie and Clyde constantly *seems* to be saying something cogent about American society, although the message has to filter through the gauze of what is presumably history, and the film's cultic following has taken it at its word. Election posters with Franklin Roosevelt's picture in red, white and blue whiz by in the background, providing the flat comparison for the vivid, intense heroes. Periodically, the gang meets up with people who have the slack-jawed bewilderment and gutted stares of the faces in a Dorothea Lange photo album; there is even a fleeting attempt to suggest Clyde's sympathy for those dispossessed and vicariously broken by Wall Street, heading West to stagnate in despairing Hoovervilles.

It is all there—but as window-dressing for fantasia. It is *not* Dorothea Lange, not even close, and it does no justice at all to the suffering she chronicled. History enters *Bonnie and Clyde* as a flippant background to make the already gorgeous characters also sympathetic, to provide a seemingly real milieu as a frame for their attempts to escape the mediocrity of a shattered world. The setting is used in much the same way that the world of advertising uses backgrounds: to create more or less subliminal presumptions in favor of what they're trying to sell. Neither the makers of this film nor the makers of cigarette ads are much interested in establishing a causal connection between backdrop and product. Such logic, in fact, is the intellectual threat that their skill is hired to overcome.

The movie doesn't have much to do with the dumpy, putty-faced dame who was Bonnie Parker, or with the homosexual punk who was Clyde Barrow. It doesn't have much to do with the world these two pillaged.

And if the film hadn't been killing the weekly rotation at local theaters for so long now, one wouldn't have to go any further. But almost everybody assumes as a matter of course that it *does* have something crucial to do with our own tilting world, with today. Recently, a friend of mine in tune with such things told me: "*Bonnie and Clyde* belongs to young people today in a way no other film has since the Beatles' movies. It speaks to them. It is about their life, about the cops beating on their heads and the inertia they have to wade through."

This is a big chunk of talk, easier swallowed than chewed, like the film itself. But if it is true that *Bonnie and Clyde* belongs to "us," perhaps we should be all the more careful about what it says. One thinks of the high points, like the early sequence in which Bonnie gives Clyde's gun a coy massage before plunging with him into the film's version of an intense life. Aside from the fact that the facial mugging accompanying this gesture has overtones of burlesque and —along with the innuendoes of sexual neurosis—shows how Freudian cliches make their way into pop culture, it also says something about what is "in" this season. For the flirtation with violence, with plastic intensity and nihilism—some of the products the film is selling—is about as masturbatory as Bonnie's attraction to Clyde's gun.

One can't help but think that some white middle-class kids— who have, by and large, grown up assuming that a cop is somebody who tells you how to find a street, but still mouth the syllables of the black revolution's authentic anger—haven't yet paid the dues that could make the vocabulary legitimate and the experience anything more than voyeurism. In the same way, the Bonnie and Clyde of the movie didn't pay enough in terms of suffering to become tragic.

This is not to say that violence is not committed in untold petty ways against the generation that presumably feels great sympathy for the movie, that a portion of them don't actually know what it feels like to be clubbed and kicked. But so far it hasn't been the sort of oppressive and overt violence that would make their threats of guerrilla warfare more than cloying rhetoric; that would make talk of running guns into the ghettos and wanting the war in Vietnam to continue because it is "radicalizing" America something more than solemn romantic nonsense. And until their experience with violence shifts from subtle to blatant, from implied to achieved, the use of fetish objects—be it of blacks, who have at least earned the right to talk of guns and cop-killing and for whom Bonnie and Clyde can't be that charging an experience, or of movie violence—will continue to seem like unfortunate narcissism.

But it is obviously more than one age group or ideological persuasion that has been fixated on *Bonnie and Clyde*. Everywhere people are looking for some hint of Armageddon, like farmers hopefully studying the sky for signs of rain. And this movie seems to offer an alternative to the massive doses of cultural novocain they've been getting.

Still, that which begins by promising relief ends up as a life-deadener. However much some aspects of American life are beginning to crack and crumble, the commercialism which saw in *Bonnie and Clyde* something to immediately profit from is still perfectly toned. Nor is the movie one of those experiences that refuse to be coopted. The two glamorous desperados—a whole Capote party in themselves—have found that their new life, which began so intensely, will be frittered away; that they will wind up as the household gods who market crummy cars and unneeded fashions, sell ladies' magazines and airplane trips and finally become little more than a hair style.

From some parts of the cult come angry voices saying that this inevitably occurs to that which is potentially pure in our corrupt world. So it does. But it isn't that much of a perversion of the role Bonnie and Clyde played in the film. They were an advertiser's dream the minute they were reborn. Every new life style has a built-in con, from which it is only a short step to a racket.

ALBERT JOHNSON

◆◇◆

Penn's *Bonnie and Clyde* created such fantastic controversy among some of the New York film critics that one is taken aback by the uproar. By now, it can be assumed that most film devotees have seen the film or at least have read reviews or articles about it. A great deal of credit for the success of *Bonnie and Clyde* must be given to the

From Film Quarterly *21, no. 2 (Winter 1967–68): 45–48.* © *1967 by The Regents of the University of California. Reprinted by permission of The Regents and the author.*

writers, David Newman and Robert Benton. They have, in this single film, brought international attention to the nineteen-thirties as the era most identifiable, in its violence of mood, aesthetic excesses, and doomed romantic optimism, with our own time. By reworking the reality of a five-year reign of banditry and terror spread by Clyde Barrow and Bonnie Parker into a folk-saga of the Southwest, the writers have embellished facts with great sympathy for a world they barely knew, and endowed an essentially grim, terrible series of crimes with the sardonic humor of a Twain or O. Henry. Thus, *Bonnie and Clyde* throws all of its dramatic weight into the realm of entertainment-above-all; its moral is the same as that of its predecessors in the genre of gangster films: the criminals die quite violently. The criticisms leveled against the film are chiefly based upon the writers' constant utilization of laughter and farcical situations throughout this gore-laden story. However, it is this device that most distinguishes *Bonnie and Clyde* from all other gangster films and leaves one with a confirmed awareness that the director and the writers have deliberately created a unique pseudo-documentary style by which spectators could be entertained and astonished at the same time. It is the *romantic imagination* in this work that makes it such a distinguished American film. There are those of us who know that the real Bonnie Parker looked more like Margaret Hamilton than Faye Dunaway, and it is certain that Clyde Barrow lacked the physical attractiveness and subtle mannerisms of Warren Beatty. It is fascinating to notice how the film rearranges the stuff of life to fit into its brilliant pattern of Technicolor episodes. The original Barrow gang was larger than *Bonnie and Clyde* would have us believe, and Bonnie was a hardened creature who longed to be a coquette. The detailed performances of Dunaway and Beatty are extraordinary because they are totally imaginative (what do they care about Depression types—the dust-destiny look of a John Garfield or the slum-weary cynicisms of a Sylvia Sidney?). One recognizes their own determination to create and vivify a personal linkage to their roles, but their cleverness shows through. Still, they win an audience's affection in the first sequence of the film, playing out a round of flirtatious wisecracks on a half-deserted rural street, outrageously *modern* and amusing, as if those two lost souls were destined to meet; charming, beautiful miscreants in defiance of poverty and boredom. One should accept the spirit of romanticism at this point, for the early escapades, Clyde's inexplicable shyness at love-making and the meeting with C. W. Moss (Michael J. Pollard) are all permeated with the picaresque spirit of adventure and frolic. The character of Moss is a masterstroke by the writers: an embodiment of back-country slyness and puckish truculence that is transformed into unforgettable humanity by Pollard. When he confronts Bonnie and Clyde with an air of suspicion and curious disbelief, turning roundabout with involuntary delight, and finally riding off with them in rumble-seat triumph, one knows that he has beheld an original talent.

Great attention is given to period details. The old automobiles, clothing, and furnishings are pretty much in order, except, as expected, with Dunaway. The blame should not be placed upon Theodora Van Runkle, who designed the costumes, but upon those who have always insisted that leading ladies must never be dressed or coiffed *entirely* in the mode of an earlier period. But Bonnie's persistent 1967 look is disturbing, and it is a flaw that Penn should not have allowed. Since the character of Blanche Barrow, Clyde's sister-in-law, is presented almost (again, *almost*) perfectly à la mode of the nineteen-thirties, it must be concluded that the glamor of the Dunaway image precluded placing her nearer to the reality of her ankle-skirted, finger-waved sisters of the past. Ironically, Dunaway would have been just as attractive if they had made her a period-figure, and it is totally out of character for Bonnie *not* to have tried to look like those Busby Berkeley girls singing "We're In The Money" in *Gold Diggers of 1933*.

Many have commented upon the sense of Americana that *Bonnie and Clyde* evokes in its imagery. This is true to a degree, but again, it must be emphasized that the camera of Burnett Guffey is guided by that nostalgic spirit which Penn insistently strengthens throughout the film. The FDR posters, Burma Shave signs, and Eddie Cantor's radio program sounding in the calm evening air; the strains of popular songs ("Deep Night," "Shadow Waltz"), all synthesize an era immediately for older members of the audience, who accept these touches and forget the past as it really was. These are very thrilling things to see in an American film, presaging an overdue movement toward neorealism in our films. The world that is shown to us is the Southwest, but often, one is confused about exact towns or states. Penn places his tragic couple in a vast network of country roads, small towns, and cheap auto courts. One shares the isolation and bickering camaraderie of the lawless quintet because

Penn draws them very close to the spectator. Gene Hackman's loudmouthed, backslapping role of Buck Barrow is a knowledgable study in insecurity and earthy humanism. A man with a single joke to tell, he brings great insight to a comic view of the American dreamer. Estelle Parson's portrait of guilt-ridden hysteria and fear makes Blanche one of the best characterizations in films for many years, in the category of Moorehead in *The Magnificent Ambersons* or Collinge in *The Little Foxes.* Her pitiful involvement with the Barrow gang represents that inexplicable, unavoidable capability for individuals to become part of a criminal way of life during the Depression, as if everyone was a potential Jean Valjean or misguided Robin Hood The bloody violence of the period was part of the law of survival, and it was not confined to the thirties; it is just that many of us who live comfortably today are unaware of, or have forgotten, the sociological urgencies and commitments of those days. By humanizing Bonnie Parker and Clyde Barrow, making them youthful, rather guileless prototypes of Depression rebels, it became easier for the film-makers to treat much of their story with humor. The folk quality is spiced by country-western breakdowns that musically celebrate Clyde's miraculous escapes from several brilliantly staged gun battles with the police; these pieces of lyricism bolster the atmosphere of fantasy which has to leaven the burden of seeing a number of policemen shot dead, and great quantities of blood pouring from wounds. But the gore is a part of folk-balladry and legend, and that is exactly what the film is about—the *legend* of Bonnie and Clyde, not the truth about them. The truthful things are in those little touches mentioned before, and in the Steinbeckian moment when an evicted farmer and his Negro sharecropper shoot the panes from the windows of his abandoned farmhouse as a futile, temporary gesture against the bank. When Clyde tells the farmer, "We rob banks," there is a priceless interchange of glances—the old man wonderingly taciturn, Clyde full of shy pleasure. And so The Bank is the Depression villain in this case, with Bonnie and Clyde as the avengers of poverty. They risk their lives, have their fun and excitement by robbing banks, the only source of money. They are classified with the noble desperadoes of filmdom: Jesse James, Joaquin Murieta, and the rest, bandits of circumstance, fighting to withstand the impersonal, cruel powers of the Railroad, the Landowners, or the Bank.

Two of the most beautiful interludes in *Bonnie and Clyde* describe
the couple's involvement with the poor. First, a haunting, dreamlike
picnic and reunion with Bonnie's relatives at an abandoned quarry
that is like an album of old color-photographs come to life. The
images are soft, misty and brief, quite timeless, with voices at a
distance—the men and women caught in the poses and movements
of casual talk or horseplay with children. Bonnie's mother, a thin,
white-haired crone, squints into the sun, resigned to death; children
roll down a slope: Clyde, white shirtsleeves aglow against his drab
vest and slouch-cap, munches an Eskimo Pie. It is a reverie by
Dorothea Lange, Walker Evans, or W. Eugene Smith. Then, another
hushed encounter becomes an exemplary sequence, defining the awe-
struck attitudes of poor people toward the lawless, thirty years ago.
Moss drives his two wounded companions to a squatters camp near a
river. The children peer into the automobile at the bloodstained
couple, whispering, "Are they *famous?*" while their elders murmur
in low, respectful voices, understanding everything and presenting
Moss with soup, water, and blankets as he departs. Help is given
humbly, tentatively, and with a touch of fear and regret.

The sense of melancholy behind the ribald escapades in *Bonnie
and Clyde* is ever-present. The bandits seldom accumulate enough
money to justify their risks ("Well, times is hard," says Buck when
Clyde wryly looks at the amount of their haul); the film does not
glorify the crimes, it praises the incredible bravado and recklessness
of those who chose the criminal's way as a career and made the best
of it, regardless of the consequences. Penn's study of the nature of
violence is carried a step further in this film; the representatives of
the law are chided (farmers, bank presidents, and policemen are all
too pleased to have their pictures in the papers as "victims" of
Bonnie and Clyde), or as in the figure of Sheriff Frank Hamer
(Denver Pyle), the law is symbolized in his stern, mustachioed visage.
When Hamer is humiliated by the gang, he spits in Bonnie's face,
and Clyde's rage becomes his most outspoken challenge to law and
order. Hamer is treated as a *force,* a more terrifying version of
Brando's sheriff in *The Chase,* a human god in khaki, indomitable
and vengeful. (In reality, Hamer's frustrations were more complex:
an ex-Texas Ranger, he was embittered and nonheroic. He became
obsessed by the elusiveness of the Barrow gang and vowed to destroy
them because of their wanton murders of police officers. The episode

in the film never happened because Hamer never caught up with Bonnie and Clyde until the final ambush, when no words were exchanged.)

Some very pleasant sequences: Bonnie and Clyde kidnap two lovers and take them for a joyride, expressing the bandits' loneliness and deeply felt need to be involved with "Jus' folks"—there is great warmth in this episode, despite Penn's tendency to let the man (Gene Wilder) overplay his polite apprehensions. When the bandits meet C. W. Moss's father (Dub Taylor), the film offers another fine character: a bully with a streak of homespun geniality, he is not as starstruck by Bonnie and Clyde as his son, and he becomes the grizzled Judas of this tale.

The dénouement is touched with a grotesque, visual poetry. Bonnie and Clyde have solved their sexual incompatibility. (This aspect of the film is unduly sensationalistic and contrived—in reality, Bonnie loved another member of the gang, not shown in the film, and actually, she was simply not Clyde's kind of woman. The implied homosexuality of Clyde is also of dubious origin and clumsily handled in terms of clarifying his personality.) They have gained national attention through their crimes and Bonnie's doggerel verse in the newspapers, and on their last ride together, they are like any fresh, country-healthy couple. When Hamer's posse riddles their car with bullets, the twitchings of death are punctuated by a slow-camera glance at Bonnie's blond hair cascading in an arc, and of Clyde rolling gently across the ground. This is not too much blood, and deep silence settles at the death of a legend.

Again, one must turn to reality: Bonnie and Clyde were ready for an ambush when they were killed on that country road in Louisiana, for both of them died holding guns. Bonnie had a machine gun in her lap, and Clyde was clutching a sawed-off shotgun as he drove. He had $507 on him and one lens was shot out of his colored glasses; Bonnie was wearing a red dress, red shoes, and a red-and-white hat, and it was discovered that she had a tattoo on her thigh. Over 167 bullets were pumped into the car, and nestled among the guns and ammunition in the back seat was a saxophone and some sheet music.

The legend clashes gently and movingly with the real. Arthur Penn's backward glance is filled with beauty and affection for an era, and there is so much talent involved in this film that his *Bonnie and Clyde* will remain an outstanding piece of cinema art, recreating social history in terms of today's acceptable myths. Above all, the mystery of Clyde Barrow and his woman accomplice remains intact. Warren Beatty has become an actor of undeniable importance with his performance here (an indelible moment, when, feelings hurt by Bonnie's sharp tongue, he stands in a field with arms raised against his chest, fists ineffectually clenched), but one still wonders about Bonnie's tattoo, and the lost notes of Clyde's saxophone, sounding old tunes in those lonely Texas nights, ages ago.

ESSAYS

The Artistic Power of
BONNIE AND CLYDE
by JOHN G. CAWELTI

Bonnie and Clyde was one of the major American artistic achievements of the '60s. Its power to move audiences deeply was apparent from its first showing, and, at least for me, several further viewings have not dissipated the film's original impact. On the contrary, fuller acquaintance with the film has shown me new elements of interest and value. No critic can be certain how future cultural changes will transform the way a contemporary work of art is understood and valued, or how much his own contemporaneous preoccupations and attitudes cause him to overvalue or find excessive interest in things that turn out to have only a momentary significance. Nevertheless, I am confident that *Bonnie and Clyde* is more than a passing fashion and will eventually be regarded (along with movies such as Welles's *Citizen Kane,* Ford's *My Darling Clementine,* Hawk's *The Big Sleep,* Griffith's *Birth of a Nation,* and Chaplin's great comedies) as one of the major classics of the American film.

The extraordinary power of *Bonnie and Clyde* has three main sources: first, the compelling drama of its story; second, the highly effective cinematography; and finally, the relation of a traditional American fantasy of violence and outlawry to the ambiguities and conflicts of feeling stemming from a central problem of American values—the clash between the belief in social order and the ideal of the totally liberated individual.

The richness and power of the story of *Bonnie and Clyde* as shaped by writers Benton and Newman and director Arthur Penn depends on the complex integration of five major narrative strands that support and intensify each other as the film develops. First, we have the basic drama of the rise and fall of gangsters, a story having such deep roots in the modern American imagination that it has inspired as many important American films as any other subject. When effectively done, the gangster film has much of the rhythm and shape of tragedy. A character of impressive force and personality rises to power and importance through actions that in turn become the cause of his destruction. Increasingly arrogant as he becomes more successful, the gangster hero finally overreaches himself and his doom catches up with him, usually in a police ambush. Thus, the gangster and his story effectively dramatize at least two important aspects of tragedy: the extreme nature of the hero's rise and fall (as Aristotle suggests, the intensity of the hero's change from happiness to misery is one basic source of our feeling for him) and the sense of inevitable fate or doom that increases our sense of the protagonist's predicament and our sympathy for him.

There is still another aspect of tragedy that the gangster can embody more effectively than any other contemporary figure. Though it is probably not necessary for the tragic hero to be a king or aristocrat, most of the great tragic protagonists of the past have been such. Modern writers have found it difficult to create powerful tragedies with salesmen or corporate executives as protagonists. I would suggest two reasons for this. In order for us to feel the full impact of the fate the hero brings on himself, he must have a nearly complete freedom of action. In other words, the more we feel the hero has been able to choose his course of action without restriction, the more we sense the tragic irony of his choices. Secondly, it seems important that the tragic hero's actions have some deep moral significance. The classic dramatists generally dealt with protagonists whose actions were lived out in a public arena. As kings or aristocratic leaders, the significance of their every action and statement could be symbolized for the audience in the response of the chorus, or in the Elizabethan plays, by a group of retainers and courtiers.

Modern democratic societies no longer accept the kind of absolute kings whose personal choices are matters of basic public import. Of course, our leaders have great political power, but it is interesting that few contemporary writers and dramatists have sought to make tragic figures of our presidents and legislators. Although these personages lead public lives that might be dramatized in the manner of classical tragedy they rarely are. Perhaps our concept of power in a democracy implies that personal impulses cannot be erected into commands without taking account of the many diverse groups whose consent is necessary to the exercise of power. Therefore we feel that our leaders lack that total freedom of action that the tragic protagonist seems to require. Whatever the reason, our political leaders have not proved promising subjects for this kind of drama. The tragedy of the salesman, on the other hand, lies in the fact that he has neither freedom of action nor public significance. This may indeed be sad, but it does not arouse the same kind of feeling as the classic tragedies.

Strangely enough, one figure in modern society who does come close to symbolizing the freedom of action and public significance we have described, is the gangster. Living out his life in public with a newspaper chorus commenting on his actions, the gangster also arrogates to himself a freedom of action possessed by no other citizen. By stepping outside the law, he acts directly out of his personal impulses and thus exercises an apparent freedom of action denied to even the most powerful political leaders. Of course, this freedom is only apparent. In actuality the gangster's spontaneous, lawless acts bring about his ultimate capture and destruction. But the ironic relation between the appearance of freedom and the inevitability of fate is precisely one of the great effects of classic tragedy.

Robert Warshow, in his brilliant essay on the gangster film, suggests one further dimension of the gangster tragedy that has a special relevance for modern American culture. This is the sense in which the gangster tragedy is in its initial movement an ironic parody of the American dream of success. The gangster protagonist, Warshow suggests, can become an embodiment of our own ambiguous feelings about the drive toward success, a conflict of feelings that is resolved in his tragic fall.

The second strand of *Bonnie and Clyde* is perhaps the most controversial element of the film: the striking use of comic effects that partly resemble the slapstick cops-and-robbers tradition of the silent film and partly suggest even older traditions of country humor and the tall tale. The film's wild car chases often have the exuberant chaos of the Keystone Kops. During the gang's first successful bank robbery, C. W. Moss, like a good law-abiding citizen decides to park his car along the curb. When Bonnie and Clyde come rushing out, they run toward the place where they had left the car and then discover it is gone. When they finally see where C. W. had parked it and hurriedly climb in, they discover that the car is wedged between other cars in front and back. The effect of chaos and incongruity is hilarious until the comedy turns to horror when, because of the delay in the escape, an elderly teller is able to leap onto the running board. Utterly panicked and out of control, Clyde shoots the old man, whose face "explodes in blood" in a sudden moment of shock and horror. A later scene, the second successful bank robbery, is even more exuberantly comic in its representation of the chase. Cars sweep down the road and out into a field, doubling back on each other, narrowly missing a total crash, in a fashion quite reminiscent of the hilarious final chase in W. C. Fields's *The Bank Dick.*

In addition to the slapstick of the chase, the film contains many other elements of buffoonery. When Clyde embarrassedly reveals his impotence after Bonnie's passionate advances, he bumps his head on one side of the car and pratfalls out of the other. Both C. W. Moss and Buck Barrow are played in part as country bumpkins, while Blanche is a hilarious representation of the genteel pretensions and hypocrisies of a preacher's daughter. Surely, few works of art with a basically tragic import have occasioned so much laughter.

This weaving together of comic and tragic elements has been strongly criticized as inconsistent and confused in tone. However, critics who liked the film, Pauline Kael and William J. Free, for instance, felt that the comedy works to soften up the audience and make the tragic eventuation even more shocking. These critics argued that the film took a rather decisive turn from comedy to seriousness about midway in its development. Thus, for them, the film was not confused because it began as a comedy and then turned into a tragedy. Although there is a powerful and controlled movement in the film from laughter to shock, the critics' conception of a decisive turn from comedy to tragedy does injustice to the mutually intensifying way these two strands are woven together throughout the film. *Bonnie and Clyde* is not wholly comic at the beginning; nor do the comic elements drop out altogether in the second half. Although the protagonists set off on their career of crime on a note of comic exuberance, premonitions of doom surround them, at first subtly and symbolically and then more explicitly. For example, intimations of tragedy crop up strikingly during the scene at the deserted farmhouse where Bonnie and Clyde sleep after their first day together and their initial crimes. As the sequence begins Bonnie awakes and is momentarily afraid, but when Clyde comes in her delight returns. But, as the two step outside in the morning sun, however, we hear the wind blowing ominously in the bushes, a sound not unlike that we will hear later and louder at the ambush. Clyde gleefully begins to teach Bonnie how to shoot, and when a farmer arrives and tells them that the bank has taken his farm, Clyde shoots up the bank's sign and then offers his gun to the farmer. The moment is full of ironies. First, the pistol shooting is intercut with a shot of the farmer's child, cowering in terror in its mother's arms from the terrible noise of the gun. Then, feeling he has established a kind of sympathetic contact with the farmer, Clyde tells him, "We rob banks." There follows a close-up of the farmer's face, suddenly withdrawn and ambiguous, an expression offering a complex but unmistakable judgment on the unrealistic fantasies of Bonnie and Clyde.

Just as there are intimations of tragedy from the beginning, comic elements are present to the end. In one of the last scenes between Bonnie and Clyde, Clyde has a terribly funny, though deeply ironic line. When Bonnie asks him whether he would do things any differently if they could walk away free from their present predicament, Clyde replies:

> Well . . . I guess I'd do it all different. First off, I wouldn't live in the same state where we pull our jobs. We'd live in one state and stay clean there, and when we wanted to take a bank we'd go to another state.

For by this point in the film, we realize that Clyde's exuberant lack of awareness of the implications of his decisions and actions has brought him to the point of destruction. It is altogether in line with this integration of comedy and tragedy that Clyde drives into the terrible ambush of death in his stocking feet, with one lens of his sunglasses out, and that the man who betrays Bonnie and Clyde to their ruthless pursuers is C. W. Moss's father, a comic old farmer who seems far more upset by C. W.'s tattoo than by his crimes.

Besides intensifying the film's tragic effect, certain elements of broad comedy play an important role in characterization. Clyde's character is tinged with a streak of clownish awkwardness and insouciance that helps to relate him to the almost completely comic portrayals of C. W., Buck, and Blanche. Although Clyde is capable of striking delicacy of feeling and perceptiveness in his relationship with Bonnie, his total insouciance and dedication to his profession, his awkward limp, his pratfalls and his childlike mixture of bravado and uncertainty immediately establish him as a special kind of figure with a mythical dimension. This mythic quality is enormously important, for a completely serious treatment of this character, with his dependence on guns and his impotence, might easily have made him simply another of these neurotic criminals who appear in gangster films like Corman's *Machine Gun Kelly*. By skillfully employing the devices of comedy, Penn creates a character who is simpler and more direct in his psychological characteristics than many other gangster heroes, yet more complex and more powerful in his effect.

These elements of comedy and tragedy are woven together by the third important strand of the *Bonnie and Clyde* story, a strand that is the most importantly distinctive and unifying element of the film: the representation of Bonnie's tragic and mistaken quest for some measure of human dignity. Bonnie is the true protagonist of the film; it is her sense of frustration and entrapment that appears at the very beginning; it is her response to Clyde's fantasy of wealth and power that creates the Barrow gang. It is she who decides to stay with Clyde when she could have gone home free after the initial robberies, and it is she who is most strongly aware of their impending death. Bonnie's poem is the one significant attempt either character makes to gain some larger awareness of his life. Finally, we see that Bonnie is able both to imagine some alternative and better fate and to accept willingly her death with Clyde. In many ways, then, the film is structured around the series of decisions and actions that lead Bonnie from her tawdry bedroom to a terrible death, along with the growing awareness and realization that this movement involves. Moreover, this movement is presented in such a way that it can be understood as being motivated by a mistaken but fundamentally serious quest for the common human goal of dignity and fulfillment.

With this in mind, another way in which the comic treatment of character is appropriate to the film becomes clear. Since the film is concerned with Bonnie's attempt to achieve dignity, it is important that the film clearly define the degrading or comic limitations of the other characters. For example, there is the indignity of being trapped in a restrictive social role—say that of a waitress in a cheap café—with little chance of escape. This is Bonnie's predicament at the beginning of the film; however, she is far more acutely sensitive to the indignity and frustration of such a situation than such characters as the older waitress who briefly appears in an early scene. Blanche Barrow illustrates a related form of indignity with more comic implications. Blanche would love to lose herself in the restrictive patterns of lower-middle-class respectability. Instead she becomes accidentally involved in antisocial actions that are the very opposite of her wishes. Even though she is forced out of her conventional role into its opposite, her awareness of the world remains as restricted as before. She responds to her situation by doing her best to live out her conception of respectability and domesticity within it; but her role of the helpless, passive female, her scorn for Bonnie's unrespectable relation to Clyde, and her insistence on being a preacher's daughter are hopelessly incongruent. Blanche's attempt to preserve her limited and demeaning social role in the midst of the gang's chaotic flight effectively sets off the seriousness of Bonnie's struggle for a new and richer sense of herself.

The characterization of C. W. Moss and Buck Barrow reveals another sort of comic indignity. These figures have rejected the role of respectable law-abiding citizen, but not as a result of conscious moral choice. Their human restriction is a form of ignorance. They don't really know the difference between a life of crime and one of honesty. C. W. is almost moronic; he is dazzled by the energy and spirit of Bonnie and Clyde. Totally wrapped up in the automobiles he fixes and drives, he follows along without thought or doubt. Even at the end, he cannot believe that the police could successfully destroy his idols. Buck, on the other hand, is a character who requires excitement and movement. Crime is not a purpose for him, but simply a way of keeping things happening. Both C. W. and Buck seem completely fulfilled in the gang's life. In a sense, they achieve a kind of personal meaning in what they are doing and consequently are never discontented. But they fulfill such a limited range of human potentialities that they remain subhuman. Their very names (Buck and Moss) suggest their radical limits as men.

Clyde is more complex in this respect. He shares Buck's and C. W.'s delight in excitement and action, and to this extent he possesses, as we have seen, a similar clownishness. Yet Clyde also has wider and higher aspirations. For him, crime does have a purpose. It is a means to the creation of a new and more significant role for himself, a role associated with his fantasies of wealth and power. He needs to be known as a person, to be the center of public attention.

His impotence can probably be best understood as an expression of the sense of anonymity and obscurity he reveals when he dreams aloud to Bonnie about the fame and fortune that awaits them. Only when his legend as a popular hero has been articulated in Bonnie's poem is he able to consummate the love he has increasingly felt for her.

This aspiration raises Clyde to a level of humanity beyond the comic ignorance of C. W. and Buck and the pathetic role-playing of Blanche. Yet, for all his attractiveness, Clyde's quest for dignity through crime remains a limited and perverse thing because of the essential childishness and superficiality of his motives. Clyde's dream of fame is on the one hand a terribly limited one that reaches its pathetic climax in a vision of walking with Bonnie into a fancy restaurant. On the other hand, it is a childish vision of omnipotence and freedom unchecked by any knowledge or acceptance of the limits of reality:

> You and me travelin' together, we could cut clean across this state, and Kansas, too, and maybe dip into Oklahoma, and Missouri and what not, and catch ourselves highpockets and a highheeled ol' time.

This is the fantasy that Clyde spells out for Bonnie at the beginning of the film, and it remains unaffected by reality until his death. Clyde does become a newspaper legend and this is important to him. Yet if we can refer to the limitations of Buck and C. W. as comic ignorance, Clyde remains a figure of tragic ignorance who cannot imagine a life deeper and richer than the temporary notoriety of the public enemy. Dazzled by his utterly insouciant sense of his own omnipotence and still childishly ignorant of any deeper sense of human good and evil, he passes from the scene with the same bemused but destructive innocence he had at the beginning of the film. Possibly, we sense some final awareness of a grown-up reality that has always eluded him, as his blasted body reaches out for Bonnie at the end.

At the beginning of the film, Bonnie, too, is easily captured by Clyde's childish fantasies of liberation and omnipotence. But at the same time her compelling need for sexual release has opened her to experience and self-questioning beyond Clyde's limitations. Again, in this connection, Clyde's impotence symbolizes the completely enclosed and self-regarding world he lives in, a closed system that he transcends, if at all, only when it is too late. But, while Clyde never reaches beyond a certain limit, Bonnie develops rather significantly in the course of the film. Her increasing awareness and depth, in contrast to the comic limitations of the other characters, make her the true center of the film, while her quest for dignity and fulfillment unifies and gives a tragic dimension to the other elements of the film.

We cannot fully understand Bonnie's development without some consideration of the fourth major strand of the story, the love of Bonnie and Clyde. For it is primarily through her developing love for Clyde that Bonnie reaches the level of recognition and awareness that gives her a tragic dignity in the fatal culmination of her flight from the tawdry room and the hopeless trap of her job as a waitress in a cheap café. Like two earlier films at least partly inspired by the story of Bonnie and Clyde—Fritz Lang's *You Only Live Once* (1937) and Nicholas Ray's *They Live by Night* (1949)—*Bonnie and Clyde* takes on something of the shape of a modern *Romeo and Juliet,* and much of the interest and success of the film, as well as many of the criticisms levelled against it, derive from its treatment of that perennially popular romantic theme, the story of doomed lovers.

The film's final power to move us lies in its successful integration of the destruction of a gangster with the human significance implicit in Bonnie's mistaken but moving search for dignity and fulfillment. To intensify our feeling for her tragedy, Bonnie must show some awareness of how she has failed, of how her fulfillment has come in the wrong way and too late to avert her inevitable destruction. Thus, one major problem for Bonnie and Clyde's creators was to make the audience feel that Bonnie had come to this awareness without breaking the limitations of the character they had created. For this reason, Bonnie's growing awareness and maturity had to be expressed largely through her relationship to Clyde rather than through any articulate formulation of her own—it being hardly conceivable that Bonnie should break into soliloquy. The development of Bonnie and Clyde's romance was a way of manifesting the tragic stature of the characters in a form consonant with their own inarticulateness and generally low level of conscious awareness of what is happening to them.

The initial attraction of Bonnie and Clyde to each other is essentially perverse, though understandable. Bonnie is drawn to Clyde because in her own sense of helpless frustration she is magnetized by his apparent potency, and sexually aroused by his gun and his willingness to step beyond the conventional social boundaries in which she feels so trapped. Clyde, on the other hand, needs an audience before whom he can play out his role of bandit hero. Thus, when Bonnie discovers Clyde is impotent, she can accept this, because his fantasies of power and freedom at least partly match her need. From the beginning, then, their love is based on the kind of fantasy that leads to violence and destruction in acting it out. For Clyde, this fantasy is never really replaced by a fuller human awareness, because his childish sense of omnipotence and his conception of himself as bandit hero are too strong to be qualified by his growing love for Bonnie. Even though he is finally able to share that love physically, the passing of his impotence neither leads him to a richer sense of human fulfillment nor changes his basic dream of himself as legendary hero. Only when he is assured of his fame by the publication of Bonnie's ballad in the newspaper can he accept Bonnie's love without reservation. And, as we see in a following scene, the experience of sexual fulfillment has not significantly changed him. He still blankly rejects any alternative vision of their lives when Bonnie offers him the beginnings of another less destructive fantasy.

Unlike Clyde, Bonnie continually changes and deepens as their relationship develops. At first, her interest in Clyde seems largely sexual; unlike the other men who are continually pawing at her, Clyde, with his air of impulsive spontaneity and his potent gun seems to offer a liberating sexual exhiliration. However, when she discovers that Clyde is impotent, instead of leaving, she accepts his fantasy of power and fame. Precisely because she recognizes her need for the self-image that Clyde offers her, Bonnie is forced to an initial realization of the difference between love as sexual aggression and love as mutual response and support. However, Bonnie's feelings for Clyde face a further challenge as she increasingly becomes aware of how little the realities of their lives will ever resemble their initial fantasies of liberation and power. Gradually, she understands and accepts not only the constrained and frustrating life of car and motel, hemmed in on all sides by the vapid antics of Buck and C. W., and the absurd pretensions of Blanche; she even comes to terms with the inevitable prospect of an early death. When she leaves her mother after the family picnic she knows that there is no going back.

In a scene immediately after the family picnic, the full weight of despair falls upon her. She cowers on a bed in one of those dingy motel rooms where the two have their few moments of peace and privacy, and speaks to Clyde of her misery. In dialogue that strangely echoes the famous scene between Hektor and Andromache in the sixth book of the *Iliad,* Bonnie tells Clyde that she no longer has a mother and Clyde frees her from her terrible sense of isolation by saying "I'm your family." This scene leads directly into the gun battle in which Buck is killed and both Bonnie and Clyde are wounded. For Bonnie, these episodes both intensify her sense of total dependence on Clyde and of the ultimate disaster that will overtake them. Her response is to write the ballad, which the actual Bonnie Parker apparently wrote. As it appears in the context set for it by the film, the ballad leads to the final sexual culmination of Bonnie and Clyde's love, but it also establishes the greater depth of Bonnie's tragic awareness. For Clyde, the ballad is essentially an assurance that he has achieved his fantasy of fame: an assurance indicated by his wondering statement to Bonnie, "you made me somebody." Because the ballad has imposed on the world his image of himself as outlaw hero, he can now use sexually the potency that earlier he released through aggression with his gun. But for Bonnie, the poem is something else, the articulation and acceptance of their mutual doom. In freeing her lover from his impotent anonymity by embodying his fantasy of fame in words, she is also facing for herself something that Clyde will never really know, the terrible sense of mortality and loss: "it's death for Bonnie and Clyde."

The last strand of the Bonnie and Clyde story is the public legend that grows up around the characters and its influence on their actions and motives. We see the legend forming in the interviews with bank officials and bystanders that are intercut with the scene of the second major robbery. It gathers new material to itself in the newspaper reports that the gang so avidly follows. The episodes in which Bonnie and Clyde, badly wounded, are given food and water at an Okie camp show still another phase of the developing legend— the outlaw-heroes have become, for some people, truly mythical and magical figures. Finally, the film continually shows us the effects of the legend on the central characters and their pursuers.

This final aspect of the process of legend-making, particularly as it reveals the way people become the captives of their legends and are thereby compelled to live out rituals of destruction and sacrifice, seems of particular interest to Arthur Penn. This theme played an important part in his treatment of the story of Billy the Kid in his earlier film, *The Left-handed Gun,* which, like *Bonnie and Clyde* portrayed Billy the Kid as a basically innocent character driven by poorly understood needs and impulses into acts that locked him into an inescapable ritual of crime, flight, and destruction. In both *The Left-handed Gun* and *Bonnie and Clyde* Penn suggests the extent to which the outlaw as legendary material, the public as legend-makers, and the law as agent for the execution of the sacrifice engage in a perverse collaboration with each other to satisfy conflicting social impulses toward anarchy and order. As Penn portrays him in these films, the outlaw turns to violence out of some perverted moral impulse and then becomes the actor in a public drama he cannot escape. Thus, by accepting the role of legendary bandit, he also becomes a kind of public agent who cannot resign his commission to act out and resolve the conflict between rebellion and authority. Although his violent crimes are surrogate expressions of the public's own anger and frustration at a sterile and restricting social environment, he, who has dared to threaten the social order, must be ruthlessly hunted down and destroyed to satisfy the public's outrage at impulses it cannot admit to itself. This interpretation of the social meaning of the outlaw legend leads to the film's emphasis on the overcharged violence and destructiveness that accompanies the hunting down and destruction of the hero. Thus, in an important sense, Bonnie and Clyde become sacrificial victims for a guilt that transcends their own crimes.

The story of Bonnie and Clyde as developed in the film thus integrates and unifies five major dramatic and thematic strands—the rise and fall of the outlaw gang, the slapstick comedy of chase and the social comedy of human eccentricity, the serious quest of an individual for dignity and fulfillment, the romantic drama of a doomed love, and the social drama of crime and its legend. Each of these strands has an interest of its own, but the special power of *Bonnie and Clyde* lies in the way they have been interrelated so that each strand is intertwined with the others in an artistic pattern that is greater than the sum of its individual parts.

II

The effectiveness with which the creators of *Bonnie and Clyde* unified a number of dramatic strands into a single coherent and moving story is central to the film's success. However, the way they employed the special resources of film to embody this story in expressive form also contributed importantly to the work's artistic power. The first necessity of effective film structure is to invent some means of creating a unified flow of movement out of many diverse segments of action and image. In dealing with this problem, the creators of *Bonnie and Clyde* seized upon one of the basic structural devices of the American film—the chase.

From the beginning, the film establishes a restless, breathless pace; our sense of the characters' situation is continually dominated by our awareness that they are on the run. The movement of cars impels us from one moment to the next, but within this basic motif a wide range of variations helps establish the tone of particular episodes and of the overall development of the film. From the wildly careening car in which Bonnie and Clyde take off after their first robbery through the slapstick car chase of the second bank robbery; from the helpless circling movement of the car around the inescapable wall of gunshots in the last big gun battle to the final slow but inexorable movement of the car into the ambush at the end of the film, the tone of the major scenes is mirrored in characteristic speeds and motions of cars.

These scenes of motion are invariably punctuated by moments of stasis, those episodes in seedy motels and run-down farmhouses in which the characters briefly rest from their inexorable flight. The content of these stasis scenes is skillfully arranged so that they become moments of confrontation in which the characters encounter the tensions between themselves and their way of life that are concealed by the frantic activity of attacking and fleeing. Dominated by Bonnie's attempt to work out her relationship with Clyde and the rest of the gang, the moments of stasis provide a basic structural means of bringing out the theme of Bonnie's quest for fulfillment, which, as we have seen, is vital to the film. The stillness of these scenes, contrasted with the incessant movement that is the dominant principle of the film, intensifies our sense of the general failure of the characters to reach any awareness of the fatality of their lives before they are impelled forward into flight again. The developing contrast of these two rhythms also represents the inescapable net in which the gang enmeshes itself. As the film progresses, the moments of stasis become progressively shorter and more quickly interrupted by scenes of violence and flight—leading up to the terrible gun

battles that result in the death of Buck, the capture of Blanche, and
the wounding of Bonnie and Clyde. After C. W. brings the badly
shot-up Bonnie and Clyde to his father's farm, there is a series of
scenes without movement. We see Bonnie and Clyde with C. W. and
his father in the farmhouse, sitting in their car and together in bed.
In some ways these are the first scenes of uninterrupted peace in
the film, just as they are the scenes of greatest intimacy and understanding between the two characters. But this is a deceptive stasis,
like the calm before the storm. Just as every other moment of stillness has been interrupted by a scene of violence and movement, the
general tranquility of the last part of the film finally erupts in the
totally chaotic movement of the ambush.

Two other important visual devices contribute to the development of this alternating rhythm. One is among the oldest structural
elements in the history of art, yet it is still oddly effective in this
case. The development of the story is accompanied by the cycle of
the seasons. Bonnie and Clyde meet in a springlike setting of fresh
sunlight and verdant foliage. As the story progresses the seasons ad-
vance through summer into fall and winter. The scene of Bonnie's
running away, of the family picnic, and of the last gunfight and
flight take place against a background of dried up cornfields, bleak
dusty landscapes, and an omnipresent wind. Even the diffuse sunshine of the picnic scene has a wintry chill about it. Finally, the
ambush ironically brings us around to the beginning. It is spring
again and the trees, bushes, and sun are reminiscent of the opening
scene; but just as the peaceful stillness of the first episodes is broken
by the crack of Clyde's revolver, the unnatural quiet of the last
scene is shattered by the ambusher's guns. The seasonal cycle intensifies our sense of the story's movement from potentiality and
possibility to death and destruction.

The second contributing visual device, the sequence of the three
major gun battles, relates to this development in a similar fashion.
The first major gun battle, in Joplin, Missouri, is still permeated
with the absurd, helter-skelter, almost comically disorganized quality
we find in the first bank robbery and in the careening car in which
Bonnie tries to make love to Clyde after the early robbery of the
grocery store. There is a tremendous amount of random movement,
a tumult of noise, including Blanche's silly screaming, incredibly
fast cuts from one fragment of the scene to another, and out of all
this confusion the gang escapes unscathed. As we shall see, the

second and third gunfights are very different in character. The different visual and emotional character of the three gunfight sequences works with the cycle of the seasons and the alternating rhythm of movement and stasis to create a larger structural pattern that bodies forth in visual terms the development of the story.

Thus far we have largely concentrated on film structure as a matter of sequential development: the problem of making one shot or sequence follow another in an interesting, expressive, and unified way, thereby creating an overall sense of rhythm and pace. We might call this, for convenience's sake, the "temporal environment" of the film, since these aspects of the film's structure shape our experience of time in the film, and, by charging the passage of time with certain meanings and emotional force, also strongly influence our response to the actions occupying that passage of time. Film also has a visual environment—the kinds of actions, objects, and settings it shows to us and the way these are composed in space. Many films fail to create expressive and distinctive visual environments; just as many do not achieve an effective method of sequential development. On the whole, these are less interesting and less effective films. A fine film works for us because its creators have managed to envision a temporal and visual environment for their action that is both intrinsically interesting and appropriate to the story.

It seems to me that one central problem the filmmakers of *Bonnie and Clyde* had to face from the beginning was attaining the appropriate balance between involvement and detachment on the part of the spectator. They achieved a balance of sympathetic identification and distance in terms of character and action: Bonnie's and Clyde's struggles for fulfillment continually engage our sympathies; Clyde's fantasies of power and his obsession with the role of bandit-hero is something most of us cannot really share. These compelling and unchanging motives make of him a more mythical and distant figure. We have also seen how the controlled contrast of the comic and the serious works in this direction. But the way *Bonnie and Clyde* treats the two basic cinematic dimensions of the temporal and visual environments also works toward this balance. The key feature of the temporal environment is involvement; the intensifying pattern of flight and its increasingly insistent movement pulls us in emotionally. The visual environment, however, seems quite brilliantly arranged to create a sense of dreamlike distance. First of all, there is the distinctive period character of the setting. Though critics have argued, probably correctly, that this is not an accurate reconstruction of the thirties, that hardly matters. Indeed, it is probably important that *Bonnie and Clyde*'s visual environment is *not* a precise reconstruction of the 1930s, for the effect is one of a vision of the past, rather than an actual past. If we see *Little Caesar* or *Public Enemy*, we see the historical past, for these films had nearly contemporaneous settings. In *Bonnie and Clyde*, however, there is a double consciousness implicit in the treatment of the historical period, just as there is in many westerns. What we see is not simply the past, but a past of the mind; it is myth rather than history, and this quality gives the visual environment of *Bonnie and Clyde* that feel of distance that balances the immediacy and involvement fostered by the temporal structure.

There are many aspects of the treatment of the film's visual environment that suggest that the mythical sense of the period is a basic element of the film's structure. There are, for example, the devices of the film's title sequence, the mixture of imitation and real photographs of the thirties, the use of a popular song with the sound so adjusted that it not only sounds like an early radio, but is played at a volume so soft that one hears it like a ghostly and haunted reminiscence of something that has passed from actuality into dream. These devices and the hushed stillness surrounding them clearly suggest some basic difference between our reality and what we are about to see. This characteristic stillness carries over into the represented spaces of the film. In the opening sequence, Bonnie and Clyde are curiously isolated in a deserted world; the main street to which they walk from Bonnie's house is empty except for one absolutely still figure of an old Negro seated on a bench. While other people increasingly appear as the film goes on, this still remains a curiously empty world in which people appear only to play their roles in the mythical drama and then disappear. Many of the small town scenes have that quality of eternal stillness out of time to be found in the extraordinary paintings of Edward Hopper. Indeed, Hopper's paintings seem to lie somewhere in the background of Penn's conception of the film's visual environment, because they not only portray similar scenes but have the same haunted quality —the visualization of an experience somewhere between dream and reality. And if some of the visual compositions of the film suggest the paintings of Edward Hopper, there is an even more direct series of visual allusions to the work of such great documentary photog-

raphers of the thirties as Walker Evans and Dorothea Lange. The
reader will, I'm sure, think of other visual allusions, or hints of
allusions, for example the reference to the bloody face in Eisenstein's
"Odessa Steps" sequence in *Potemkin* in the treatment of the elderly
cashier shot by Clyde after the first bank robbery, and the direct
quotation from Busby Berkeley's *Golddiggers of 1933* in the movie-
house sequence. The point about all these allusions is not that one
has to identify them to appreciate the film or that they provide some
special key to its meaning, but that they create a particular sense of
reality in which we experience the juxtaposition of images belonging to different historical actualities.

Thus, while the temporal environment of the film possesses a compelling and emotionally involving structure of movement and stasis,
the visual environment acts on us to create a sense of distance and
myth, implying that we are the witnesses of actions that have a
larger, more portentous significance. Of course, if the conception of
the characters and actions were not sufficiently complex and sufficiently meaningful to bear this weight, no amount of skillful
cinematic treatment would completely elevate them to a level of
tragic power. This is the point on which so many westerns ultimately
fail. But the story and characters of *Bonnie and Clyde* are successfully related to the cinematic conceptions of temporal and visual
structure. How effectively these basic conceptions generate and control particular details of the film can be shown by a more intensive
analysis of some of the particular episodes.

III

In their original script, Benton and Newman wanted the film to
begin with "two title cards introducing the central characters,
executed in the style of similar cards used to begin the serials of
the late 1930s. The title cards show a photograph of the character
looking straight ahead, posed against the plain white background."
These cards, which provided the necessary background information,
were to be followed by the credits which "should be simple and
absolutely silent. No music should occur in the film until where first
indicated in the script." [1]

[1] From Robert Benton and David Newman, *Bonnie and Clyde*, p. 1; a
mimeographed film script of 129 pages, not dated. I would like to express my
gratitude to Arthur Penn for loaning me his personal copy of this version of

Benton and Newman clearly had in mind certain essential qualities needed to establish a basic tone for the film. First, the credits would be stark, silent, and simple, in keeping with the ultimately serious quality of the film. Second, they should have a quasi-documentary quality to suggest the historical reference of the events, and finally, there would be a period quality about them to establish the feeling of a specific era in the past. As the concept of the title credits developed in the process of editing the film, these basic ideas led to a more elaborate development. The two title cards called for in the original script were retained, but in the film itself they were preceded by a series of family photographs in the style of the period representing the Barrow and Parker families during the childhood and youth of Bonnie and Clyde. These photographs were interspersed with the titles, the only sound being a loud click accompanying each photograph as it flashed on the screen. Presumably the click represented the snapping of the camera shutter, yet in the strange silence of this beginning series of photos, it had a disturbing and ominous quality. The title of the film and the names of the central actors bear out this feeling. They appear in white on a dark background and then turn red. The photographs of childhood family scenes suggest a world of innocent harmony and purity, while the sound of the camera shutter and the color change hint at the fateful events that are to disrupt this world.

There is another important function of the sequence of family photographs. The sense of a mythical past, as opposed to a purely historical representation, involves a paradoxical feeling that the events and characters represented are not limited to a specific past moment. Rather, they exist, outside of our ordinary experience of time, in a nonhistorical past that can be felt as continually present, as part of our own lives. Myth is eternally present in the sense that it embodies a pattern that is repetitive and archetypal in human life. To make us feel this eternal presence, as in a tragedy, there must be something about the work that both places it in time and delivers it from the limitations of the past. We have already discussed how some of the central characteristics of the visual environment of *Bonnie and Clyde*—the slightly-off period styles, the strangely empty streets—contribute to the feeling of events that are

---

the script for study. This same basic conception of the title footage was retained in the final script, dated September 9, 1966, and was evidently changed in the process of shooting and editing.

both in and out of the past. The family photographs that open the film have a similar effect. They are clearly material of the past and yet, as family photographs, they partake of that universal American habit of collecting important moments in albums. The device is strongly effective, evoking in some fashion our own childhoods and the old family photographs treasured by parents and grandparents. Arousing our personal nostalgia for lost innocence, yet undercutting that feeling with the austere and foreboding manner in which the photographs are presented, the opening credits effectively work toward that strange and haunting moment in which, from a distance we hear as if over an old radio or phonograph, one of the popular lovesongs of the thirties, "Deep in the Arms of Love." The song is like a ghostly presence, hovering in the air, out of the past, yet heard in the present. With this striking use of sound to bear out the sense of mythical time created visually by the sequence of photographs, the two title cards describing Bonnie and Clyde appear, and the film is ready to begin. By adding the period photographs and the popular song to Benton's and Newman's original idea of the simple title cards, the final film version greatly augments the viewer's sense of personal contact with the world of the film without destroying the semidocumentary quality and the austere simplicity originally sought by the scriptwriters. Indeed, this is one of the major lines along which Penn sought to shape the film; whereas Benton's and Newman's original conception is somewhat divided between sympathetic involvement and an emphasis on the curious and even perverse aspects of the characters, Penn achieves a more coherent tragic development, eliminating the conflict between sympathy and distaste by establishing the characters in a mythical dimension of experience. Because the opening credits establish this sense of an archetypal rather than a documentary past and the rest of the film maintains it, we are able to become fully involved with the central characters, to feel their fate with great immediacy. Yet because they are mythically distant from us, we are partially released from the need to make moral judgments on their actions.

The film itself begins with a lap dissolve from Clyde's title card to an extreme close-up of a pair of lips, accompanied by the last bars of "Deep in the Arms of Love." [2] In this context, the fading

[2] Those familiar with film history will recall the striking cut to an extreme close shot of Kane's lips as he speaks his dying word, "Rosebud," in the opening

out and in of successive images effectively carries out the motif of mythical distance. Yet, though the lap dissolve maintains the quality of distance, the gradual emergence of a pair of immense lips with a lipstick being brushed across them has a tremendous impact of sensuous immediacy and sexuality. There is something vulgar and common, perhaps even slightly obscene about the application of the lipstick. As Benton and Newman indicate in their script directions, Bonnie "is standing before the full-length mirror in her bedroom doing her make-up. She overdoes it in the style of the time: rosebud mouth and so forth." However, while the vulgar, period quality called for by the script is there, other elements of the scene as filmed strongly qualify that response. Most importantly, the perspective Penn gives us on the scene makes it impossible for us to see it simply as the representation of a vulgar girl putting on lipstick in the style of the period. Because the shot begins with an extreme close-up and then withdraws first to show us a mirror image of Bonnie's face and then the back of Bonnie's head as she looks in the mirror, our own relationship to Bonnie is structured from the outset in a particular fashion. Our first experience is neither of a character nor of a character's perspective; it is our own immediate perception of a pair of warmly sensuous lips experienced directly because we do not yet see a character to attach them to. Thus, after the opening credits have established a sense of the mythical past, we become immediately involved in the experience of that past and of the sensuous force it contains. Then, before we pull back to a more objective view of the character, we are momentarily given a sense of her perspective as she views herself in the mirror. Thus, from the opening shot we get a complex sense of Bonnie as a character; she is a figure from the past, vulgar, common, and limited, the type of girl who puts on too much make-up; yet she also represents a powerful sensuous force, immediately attractive and compelling. We find ourselves involved with her in a powerfully intimate fashion.

The central artistic problem of the opening sequence of the film, which runs from the beginning to the first robbery and escape, was to motivate at a rather breathless pace the initial encounter and involvement of Bonnie and Clyde. Given the situation, this might

---

sequence of *Citizen Kane*. The effect of this cut in *Bonnie and Clyde* is very different, however, because of its different context.

seem an impossible feat: we are asked to believe that a girl who first sees a man when he attempts to steal her mother's car would run away with him after little more than five minutes' acquaintance.

Initially, three major qualities of Bonnie are made clear: her sense of frustration, her impulsive sensuality, and her naïveté. In addition, to prepare us for the appeal Clyde makes to her social aspiration after his sexual impotence has been revealed, the images hint at more complex aspirations on Bonnie's part. The first two minutes of the film brilliantly create these feelings. By shot-angles and camera movements working in combination with the gestures and movements of Faye Dunaway, Penn conveys the sense of a caged spirit aching for release. After the opening shot at the mirror, Bonnie restlessly stands up and looks around her room and then throws herself down on her bed. The camera pulls back slightly from its earlier close-up to reveal her head and shoulders. Tilted up to do so, the shot emphasizes the ceiling and walls of her room as they oppressively surround her. Another sudden movement and we see that Bonnie has flung herself down on the bed. For a brief moment, we are slightly disoriented, and this increases our sense of the impulsiveness of the movement. Again, the camera moves in on a tighter close-up, showing Bonnie looking between the bars of her bed, emphasizing again the images of constraint and imprisonment. Then, we move in still further on an extreme close-up of Bonnie's eyes, which, in this context, look like they are imprisoned in her flesh. The effect of frustration is quite overpowering, yet it also reminds us of the earlier close-up of Bonnie's lips, which confronted us directly with her intense sensuality. The next cut gives us a medium shot of Bonnie as she goes behind a screen to get dressed, passing by her dresser, which is covered with little figurines and a doll.

Although many of the basic elements remained the same, shooting and editing transformed this opening from the description in the script:

> The bedroom itself is a second-story bedroom in a lower-class frame house in West Dallas, Texas. The neighborhood is low income. Though the room reveals its shabby surroundings, it also reveals an attempt by Bonnie to fix it up. Small and corny *objets d'art* are all over the tops of the bureaus, vanity tables, etc. (Little glass figurines and porcelain statuettes and the like.)
>
> Bonnie finishes admiring herself. She walks from the mirror and moves slowly across the room, the CAMERA moving with her, until

she reaches the screened window on the opposite wall. The shade is up. There are no curtains. She looks out the window, looking down, and the CAMERA looks down with her.[3]

This description emphasizes two things: the tawdry shabbiness of Bonnie's environment together with the pathos of her vulgar attempts to dress it up, and the rather complacent and lazy narcissism of Bonnie's character. These elements remain in the scene as shot and edited, but they become distinctly subordinate to our sense of a powerful sensuality tormented by its imprisonment in a room and in a role. Notice how the specific social characteristics that place Bonnie in a particular social milieu stand out in the description, but seem far less important in the film. The "small and corny *objets d'art*" through which Benton and Newman sought to express Bonnie's pathetic attempts to transcend her surroundings are still part of the setting, yet Penn portrays Bonnie's desire to escape much more powerfully by giving us a close-up of her tormented eyes and by showing her striking against the bars of her bed. In terms of shots and editing, the method chosen by Penn is to use a variety of close-ups and rather sudden and impulsive cuts that do not slowly follow Bonnie's movements across the room as the script description suggests. The effect of this is to replace the rather catlike self-satisfaction that seems to be the image called for in the script by a much more intense and impulsive set of feelings. On the whole, the actual film gives us a deeper and more complex sense of Bonnie as a woman of great sensuous vitality and urgency hemmed in by a restrictive setting whose limitations she strongly feels.

At this point, Bonnie and the viewer get their first shot of Clyde. Bonnie has gone behind a screen to dress when she notices something outside the room. As we follow the line of her attention, the film cuts to a long shot through the window that shows Clyde beginning to tinker with a car. Bonnie comes to the window and there is an exchange of shot-angles: Clyde looking up at Bonnie and Bonnie looking down at Clyde. These shots establish the immediate sense of magnetism and attraction between the two. The outdoor long and middle shots reveal a lovely bright springlike day and set up a strong contrast with the suffocating close-ups and medium shots inside

---

[3] From Robert Benton and David Newman, *Bonnie and Clyde*, p. 2; mimeographed screenplay of 134 pages, dated September 6, 1966 and labelled "Final." This opening sequence of the film is reprinted at the end of this anthology.

Bonnie's room. The attraction of the open air and sunshine intensifies our sense of the closed-in room and Bonnie's inner need to escape from the limits of her restricted life. Again the motif of sensuous needs pushing against the shabby confines of her room is carried out in the shots of Bonnie, who is naked, standing in the window looking down on Clyde. Bonnie's few words to Clyde:

Hey, boy! What you doin' with my mama's car?

are wonderfully belied by the way she stands temptingly draped across the window. A tremendous force is impelling Bonnie toward Clyde and their byplay as they size each other up nicely fits the description in the script:

Already they are in a little game, instigated by Bonnie, sizing each other up, competing in a kind of playful arrogance. Before they speak, they have become co-conspirators.

With a quick "Wait there!" Bonnie turns to throw on her dress and rush down the stairs. Penn shoots Bonnie coming down with an almost grotesquely angled shot up the dark stairway. We see a long dark passage with light at the top. The figure of Bonnie appears at the top and rushes down on the camera with a great clumping and clattering sound. The effect of this shot is both emotionally and symbolically important. It suggests tremendous intensity and haste as well as a kind of pell-mell awkwardness that effectively represent Bonnie's feeling as she runs from her room to meet Clyde. The symbolic overtones are important too. The angle of the shot necessarily emphasizes the ugly and distorted quality of Bonnie's movements at this point; there is a comic awkwardness about this way of seeing a woman come down the stairs as well as a sense of foreboding and strangeness about the darkness of the stairway. The act of coming down the stairs becomes charged with the implications of descent and fall, of Bonnie's entering a dark passage. Again, a particular shot brings out the mythical overtones of the film.

The next series of shots portray the first direct encounter between Bonnie and Clyde on the same level. After her rush down the stairs, Bonnie comes through the door of her house and onto the porch. The camera cuts from the long upward shot in the stairway to a more or less eye-level shot of the porch; we see Bonnie come through the front door and then, suddenly stop, realizing that she is about to step into something quite new. Momentarily, her pride and sense of propriety take over control of the inner urgency that drew her from her room. As the scene progresses, she and Clyde both put each other on, pretending that they are what they are not, yet revealing that each knows exactly what the other is and feels strongly attracted. Appropriately, the camera shows us much of this scene from subjective perspectives. The first series of shots are exchanges between the two. Finally, as the two come closer we have a pair of across-the-shoulder shots: Clyde seen across Bonnie's shoulder and vice versa. Only after this sequence does the camera pull away from the subjective perspective to show us the two characters from an objective angle. It is also significant that these are generally medium shots and that they are taken from a head-on perspective in contrast to the extreme close-ups and sharply angled shots of the opening. In this context, the effect of the change in shots reflects a transition from extreme inner subjectivity—the representation of Bonnie's inner frustration and urgency—to the more public and less intimate posture she puts on before Clyde. This kind of shooting and cutting back and forth between the two emphasizes such qualities as Bonnie's shyness and pride and her sense of propriety, though at the same time we realize that these are put-on qualities rather than the manifestation of Bonnie's actual inner spirit and needs.

The initial sparring of Bonnie and Clyde concludes with Clyde's invitation to walk with him into town. Bonnie accepts, but covers her eagerness by the flip comment "Goin' to work anyway." At this point, the camera technique changes from the alternating subjective shots of the preceding sequence to a tracking two-shot, following the pair as they walk toward the center of town, Bonnie leading the way. The tracking is effective for a number of reasons. First, the film's rhythm depends on both a continual sense of movement and an alternation of moments of stasis with impulsive and rapid motion. Here, the tracking picks up the motif of rapid movement already generated by Bonnie's rushing down the stairs from her room and carries it forward into town, where it will be picked up again when the protagonists flee in a stolen car after the first robbery. Second, the tracking movement represents Bonnie's emotions at this point. In moving toward town with the camera impulsively following her pace she is both moving away from Clyde and into an involvement with him. At two points the track halts and begins again, dramatically punctuating moments of doubt and hesitation in Bonnie's feeling about their relationship; the first comes when Clyde reveals to Bonnie that he has correctly identified her as a waitress, the second when he tells her he has just been in prison. In actuality, these two revelations are disturbing on the surface to Bonnie's sense of self-esteem and her residual sense of moral and social propriety, yet in a deeper sense they reflect qualities of Clyde that are part of his magnetic attraction for her. He knows who she is and, therefore, has some insight into her terrible sense of frustration. And he is a real criminal and, therefore, represents to her a possible liberation from the social trap in which she feels herself caught. The halting of the camera movement at these points suggests the inner workings of Bonnie's mind. These are moments when she is confronted with something requiring deeper reflection and decision. Her acceptance of Clyde's immediate grasp of the fact she is nothing but a waitress signals us that her attraction to Clyde is stronger than her sense of pride, although her immediate reaction is to get back at him by asking what he does when he's not stealing cars. When Clyde tells her he has been in state prison, the track again halts, revealing the surprise and excitement this idea has for Bonnie, though she covers up again by an attempt at sarcasm.

A cut brings the two into town with another track. Several important changes in the shot subtly express the psychological currents that are increasingly drawing the two together. The change in background and lighting is extremely important. We have seen Bonnie and Clyde walking down a bright, sunny street, with a background of light, white houses, and trees. As they enter the main street of town, they come into a strangely lit, closed-in, seemingly deserted space. We have already commented on the mythical quality of this deserted town. It also connotes a social desolation that is part of the background of depression and misery that recurs throughout the film, playing an important part in shaping our sympathies for the main characters. As we enter this scene, the camera is much further away from the two characters. As if in response to the emptiness around them, we see them as smaller and closer together. The earlier track showed Bonnie leading the way, with Clyde tagging along behind, but, in this shot, Clyde gradually moves from his position in the rear to the foreground. When he tells Bonnie about cutting off his toes and offers to take off his shoe and show them to her, the camera moves in and we see Clyde in medium shot with Bonnie behind him. The respective positions and movements of Bonnie and Clyde, and the angle and distance from which they are shot, nicely express the growing inner attraction between them, intensified by our sense of them as the only live figures in a totally dead town. In addition, the isolation from other human contacts is striking. This absence of society suggests a curiously inverted Garden of Eden, with Bonnie and Clyde as newly created beings suddenly thrust into an empty world. This isolation continues continues for several minutes until after the first robbery and Bonnie's unsuccessful attempt to arouse Clyde sexually. A number of details seem at least partly calculated to evoke some of the resonance of this traditional symbolism: Bonnie as a naked Eve in her bedroom; the cokes they offer each other (apples of knowledge); and the sudden intrusion into the primal stillness of violence and sexuality. While the use of this symbolism is never obtrusive, it does work effectively, with the lovely freshness of the natural light and ambience of the scene in front of Bonnie's house, to create a sense of naïveté and innocence that is an important aspect of the characters of Bonnie and Clyde. Because this quality of youthful isolation and freshness hovers about the initial meeting of the two characters, we never quite forget it. It remains as a sense of loveliness destroyed and perverted but never completely eliminated.

The next brief scene—the coke drinking—is the climactic moment of the opening episode because it moves the drama from the initial mixture of mutual attraction and sparring for position between the two characters into violent action—the first robbery and flight. In essence, the function of the scene is to bring Bonnie's interest in Clyde to a point of high tension, to project her general frustration into a specific sexual urgency, and then to show how an essentially creative sexual interest can be perverted into a fascination with violence, thereby making Bonnie a willing accomplice in Clyde's crimes. The scene begins with a quick dissolve from the preceding scene of Clyde and Bonnie together on the street to a tight close-up of Clyde. Although relatively brief, the scene is cut with great intricacy and played out primarily in close-ups, a structure that gives it a feeling of great intensity and portent. The action is relatively simple. Clyde and Bonnie drink cokes and talk briefly about robbery. Bonnie scoffs at Clyde's actually being capable of armed robbery and Clyde shows her his gun. Then, after her remark that he "wouldn't have the gumption to use it," Clyde goes across the street to rob the grocery store. Penn makes this brief scene fully expressive of the complex inner action of sexual attraction and its projection of violence. The opening close-up of Clyde, shot at an upward angle, is expressive of striking vigor and potency with the upward projection of the coke bottle breaking across the semicircular rim of Clyde's hat, and the little matchstick sticking out of Clyde's mouth at another angle. Cutting quickly to a close-up of Bonnie's face, we see her across Clyde's upturned face, partly framed by that phallic coke bottle, her own coke dangling down from her lips as she looks up with barely disguised interest at Clyde. After these striking opening shots, the next pulls back to mid-range to establish the scene, showing the two figures at a gas station where they bought the cokes. Next follows an exchange of close-ups, strikingly shot from directly behind the cheek of the other figure so that we see a portion of Clyde's face slightly out of focus and across that a full-face close-up of Bonnie and vice versa. We feel some of that same intimacy and intensity that characterized our opening view of Bonnie in her room, as if the underlying urgencies of that scene had come to the surface again. When Clyde takes out his gun, we have the following sequence of shots:

1. Mid-range two-shot across Bonnie, who is in the foreground, onto Clyde, who is taking out his gun from inside his jacket. The angle here represents Bonnie's perspective, yet at the same time enables us to see her mixed feelings of attraction and repulsion expressed by the half turn of her body toward Clyde.

2. Tight close-up of Bonnie's face as her expression shifts from the slightly lifted eyebrows and smile (mild scoffing) of the previous close-ups to one of intense interest and excitement.

3. Close-up of Clyde's hand holding the gun, slightly concealed behind the coke in his other hand. The obvious association of coke and gun as phallic symbols, though almost blatantly simple-minded when verbalized seems much less pat and more natural when seen in visual images.

4. Close-up of Clyde's head seen in profile. The match he has been holding in his teeth dances up and down. By taking out his gun, he has proved his point and finally asserted his dominance over the saucy Bonnie.

5. A striking two-shot from an upward angle showing Clyde's

face turned away from Bonnie in the foreground. Across that, we see Bonnie looking down at the gun, hypnotized by its attraction, yet still a bit reluctant to touch it. It fascinates her like a snake; her instinctive repulsion, which is nicely suggested by the way the shot pulls back and up from her, only makes it more compelling.

6. The same shot as "3" (above), this time with Bonnie's hand reaching in to touch the gun caressingly. As the script puts it, "The weapon has an immediate effect on her. She touches it in a manner almost sexual, full of repressed excitement."

7. Close-up of Clyde's head slightly tighter than "4," above and head-on rather than profile. The match is now at full erection, no longer dancing up and down.

8. Close-up of Bonnie's head, also head-on, with lips parted and a faraway look in her eyes, as she dares Clyde to use the gun.

9. Close two-shot of Clyde head-on across Bonnie's profile, as he turns to go across the street and rob the grocery store.

10. Extreme long shot (a striking contrast after the intense series of close-ups we have just been through) showing the main street with Clyde walking across it to the grocery store. There is a moment of silence and then we see Clyde come out followed by the store owner. Clyde fires the first shot in the film and the chase is underway.

In this sequence of shots, Penn very effectively structures the scene to bring out the complex sexual meanings implicit in the action, and, thereby, to make us understand how and why these two characters must come together in search of consummation for their urgent inner drives.

Although these opening sequences take only a few minutes of time, they are quite complex in expression of character and theme. In addition, the perspective they take on the action enforces on the viewer a complex attitude toward what he is seeing. Character, theme, and perspective are, of course, developed more fully in the course of the film. The need to break out of social and sexual confinement, which we see as so basic a motive of Bonnie's character, spills out into the driving pace of the film's structure of flight and pursuit. It is perhaps the basic energy of the film, a force that drives toward violence and passion, and ultimately to death. Yet, just as this terrible energy is qualified in the opening sequences by a comic innocence and posturing—the role of proud lady Bonnie tries to play for Clyde and the role of experienced desperado and man of the world Clyde puts on—so the desperate violence of the gang is continually mixed with comic misadventure and humorous portrayal of character. For example, Bonnie's put-on pretensions in the opening sequence are projected in more emphatic comic form in the character of Blanche. The social and moral isolation of Bonnie and Clyde remains a basic element in the film, just as the visual environment of Bonnie's room is carried through in the sequence of lonely and confined motel rooms in which the two characters work out their fate. These opening sequences are established with the special mixture of mythical distance and intimacy that continues to be a basic structural characteristic of the film—reflected particularly in the interplay between violent action portrayed as comic ballet and the terribly vivid and disturbingly close treatment of characters being wounded and killed. Finally, the urgencies of Bonnie's character, so richly expressed in the opening sequence's structure of close-ups, gestures, and impulsive movements and cuts, form the basis for the theme of Bonnie's quest for fulfillment that is so central to the film.

IV

Bonnie's and Clyde's rise and fall are defined by the ten major sequences presenting the Barrow gang's robberies, their battles with the police, and the final ambush that destroys them. Although these are usually scenes of violent action, they are conceived, filmed, and edited in such a way as to evoke an emotional progression that builds up to the tragic effect of the film.

1. The First Grocery-Store Robbery

This scene follows immediately after the opening sequence. Since the robbery is not a planned action, it carries a tone of impulsiveness and spontaneity, even a touch of gaiety. No one is hurt, only one shot is fired, and Bonnie and Clyde escape easily. There is no pursuit. Instead, the robbery scene leads immediately into Bonnie's attempted seduction of Clyde, her sexual aggression mirroring Clyde's attack on the grocery store. The scene is filmed in such a way as to minimize our sense of the moral implications of Clyde's actions, as if to make us share Clyde's inability to recognize the suffering and pain that his actions cause. At the same time, we are kept at a distance from the robbery. The scene is filmed in long shot up the empty town street. In the distance, we see Clyde cross the street and enter the store. In a moment, he rushes out, awkwardly looking back into the store. We are somewhat closer to this action, though still across the street. The store keeper comes out and Clyde fires his pistol into the air, the first loud noise of the film. The pistol shot momentarily shatters the sense of quiet and distance, but the store keeper rushes back into the store and Bonnie and Clyde gaily drive off in a stolen car to the leitmotif of the banjo music that will become an increasingly ironic accompaniment to their escapes.

2. The First Bank Robbery

In this, as in the first grocery-store robbery, nobody gets hurt and a tone of lightness and humor still predominates. This is his first bank robbery, and Clyde is nervous and jumpy; like a man who has just been promoted he faces his new responsibilities with a mixture of pride and apprehension. He and Bonnie have carefully dressed themselves for their debut and they approach the bank in a jaunty sports coupé. When Clyde first enters the bank, he is so nervous he can barely control his voice. These actions arouse our humorous sympathy for the two. When it turns out that the bank has failed and has no money, we are made even more aware of the social desolation and emptiness that characterized the town in the opening sequence. The scene concludes with a touch of domestic comedy. Embarrassed by the fiasco of the bankrupt bank, Clyde insists that the one remaining bank officer come out to the car to explain the situation to Bonnie. Bonnie breaks into spontaneous laughter, both at the irony of the empty bank and at Clyde's discomfiture. Clyde sulks. However, underneath the comedy, there is an ominous note that breaks forth into overt violence at the end of the scene. Although Clyde's stage fright is amusing, it is also upsetting because one doesn't quite know which way he is going to jump. When he gestures aggressively at the old bank teller to make him come outside and tell Bonnie of the bank's failure, there is a momentary feeling that he might actually hurt the old man, a feeling that is carried through in the next bank robbery, when Clyde actually shoots an elderly teller. Moreover, the bank's emptiness, though doubtless hinting rather ambiguously at some extenuation or justification of Bonnie's and Clyde's decision to become criminals, also foreshadows the future. This feeling is further intensified when Clyde, angered and frustrated at his failure, shoots out the bank's window and then drives furiously away, nearly running into a small truck. The ending of the scene immediately recalls the way the first robbery scene was punctuated by gunfire and a careening car. Here, however, the several gunshots, the actual destruction of a window and the near accident make us increasingly aware of the destructive potential in Clyde's impulsive spontaneity.

3. The Second Grocery-Store Robbery

This scene is almost a continuation of the preceding episode and it completes the initial turn from humor to horror. Unlike the first grocery store robbery, we see this one on the inside, in middle shots and close-ups. Although the beginning of the scene has a kind of humor about it—Clyde behaves just like a customer asking for groceries except that he holds a gun—the humor quickly turns to a scene of violence as the first blood is spilled. A large, hulking butcher comes at Clyde with a meat cleaver and, in fighting him off, Clyde first smashes him on the head with his pistol and then shoots him. The cutting and camera movements in this scene are very rapid and chaotic, involving us directly in the action, quite unlike the relative distance of the two preceding scenes. The butcher's violence is a mirror of Clyde's increasingly destructive impulses in the two preceding scenes. It begins to develop one of the film's central themes: the dialectical relationship of violence between criminal and society that leads to a tragic escalation of suffering.

4. The Second Bank Robbery

After the shocking violence of the second grocery robbery, this scene is, at first a return to the tone of gaiety and humor that dominated the first bank robbery. C. W. has been added to the gang. His moronic vacuity, combined with Bonnie and Clyde's nervousness, turn the first part of the scene into a comic pandemonium. At the beginning of the scene, Clyde and Bonnie assume the classic position of bankrobbers, but nobody pays them any attention since Clyde at first speaks too softly for anyone to hear. This beginning is juxtaposed with the incredible situation in which C. W. parks the get-away car. When Bonnie and Clyde rush out with the money, they cannot at first even see the car. After they rush to it, C. W. discovers that he has been hemmed into his parking place and must go back and forward several times to work his way out. By the time these maneuvers have been accomplished, the bank officers and police have come rushing out. An elderly teller leaps onto the car's running board and, in one of the most striking moments of the film, Clyde shoots him in the face. The power of this close-up was such that almost every critic of the film noted it, and many saw it as an important turning point. It is Clyde's first murder and it lacks even the extenuation of self-defense that was at least partly present in Clyde's beating of the butcher in the second grocery store robbery. Yet, Clyde's act is not that of a vicious killer; as always he acts impulsively and without thought in the panic of the moment. The feel of chaos imparted to the scene by rapid camera movements gives the viewer some sense of the disorientation and panic out of which Clyde acts. His momentary contrition in the movie house after the escape seems authentic in this light. Thus, the killing becomes more like a tragic deed, an action with fated consequences, committed partly out of impulse and mistake, but nonetheless a deed whose implications are now inescapable.

5. The Gun Battle at Joplin

The action of retribution begins almost immediately. After the first gun battle, there is only one more scene in which the gang is itself the attacker. From this point, the crescendo of pursuit and flight builds up. The cinematic treatment of the three major gun battles effectively reflects this mounting intensity of flight and entrapment. The final script gives the following directions:

> The three major gun battles in this film . . . each have a different emotional and cinematic quality. The quality for this Joplin debacle is chaos, hysteria, extremely rapid movement and lots of noise. The audience should be assaulted. From the moment Clyde cries out, and throughout all the following action, Blanche, in blind panic, SCREAMS hysterically. The scream persists through the gunfire, never lessening on the soundtrack. Its effect should be at first funny to the audience, then annoying, and finally terrifying.

The effect of chaos and hysteria in the Joplin battle is conveyed by a daring structure of cuts, stressing the rapidity and confusion of the action. This must be one of the most intricately edited scenes in the history of film. Although the action occupies only a few minutes, it is made up of over sixty cuts, some of them occupying only a few frames. In addition, the great majority of these are medium shots, so that we are rarely given a glimpse of the overall action of the fight. Instead we leap from one person to another and from inside to outside in a fashion that echoes the disorientation and chaos of the action. The extremely rapid cutting and the predominant use of medium shots strongly contrasts with the cinematic structuring of the other two gunfights.

Thematically, the Joplin gunfight is the point at which the Barrow gang is transformed from more or less amateur bandits to hunted, professional criminals. The next major episode grows out of the initial confrontation between the gang and Texas Ranger Frank Hamer who will plan and direct the final destruction of Bonnie and Clyde. The structure of the scene is extremely appropriate to the gang's transition into the role of public enemy. In this first major meeting between the gang and its police pursuers, both sides fall into confusion, but as the scene progresses, the gang begins to work as a unit and eventually succeeds in escaping unscathed, even picking up the hysterical Blanche on the way out of town. The structuring of the sequence effectively brings out this aspect of the action while still leaving us with the dominant image of chaotic hysteria.

As the scene begins, we are in the Joplin apartment with the gang and we see as Clyde does, the stealthy arrival of the police in a long shot through the window. This shot is an ironic echo of the long shot through the window in the opening sequence in which Bonnie sees Clyde attempting to make off with her mother's car, and is one of a number of visual parallels with that opening sequence that show what has happened to the two characters who began their relationship with such gaiety and impulsiveness. Like Bonnie's mother's house, the apartment in Joplin is a two-story white frame building, and the action flicks back and forth between the outside and the second-story window. Here, however, the exchange is gunfire rather than the teasing byplay that marked the initial conversation of Bonnie and Clyde. And whereas Bonnie descended to follow her erotic attraction to Clyde, the gang comes down to destroy and flee. What began as a quest for liberation becomes an inexorable trap.

After the initial surprise of the police appearance, the sequence moves quickly through a series of rapid cuts and tracks in medium shots showing the gang responding to the appearance of the police. These shots, which show quick glimpses of the Barrows and Moss running around in the apartment, taking up their guns, and beginning to shoot, express the surprise and confusion of the gang, effectively symbolized in an extreme form by Blanche's hysterical screams. The next part of the sequence is also a rapid series of cuts in medium shot that makes it difficult to get a clear sense of sequence and spatial orientation. This group of cuts increases the confusion of the scene by skittering back and forth between the police and the gang, between outside and inside. Despite the feeling of chaotic confusion among the participants in the gunfight, the viewer is able to follow the rising curve of action through several important structural repetitions, particularly the way the shift between indoor and outdoor shots pivots around a repeated shot of the second-story window that is blank on its first appearance and then, as the same shot is repeated several times, erupts in gunfire. In effect, this part of the gunfight scene intercuts several simultaneous actions—Clyde, C. W., and Bonnie grabbing guns and beginning to shoot, Blanche screaming, Buck preparing to make his dash out the door, the police dispersing and shooting from various angles—all tied together around the pivotal shot of the window with its ironic visual echo of the opening sequence.

Out of the mounting confusion of simultaneous, fragmentary action, there finally emerges a clear line of action, marked by an increasing use of tracking shots, some of which appear to be hand held, and by a growing predominance of long shots that give us a clearer sense of the spatial organization of what is taking place. In the cutting, the fragmented, simultaneous actions increasingly give way to the representation of this single line in which the gang work together to escape. This single line is marked both by purposive action and sheer hysteria. While Buck is rushing out of the apartment to release the brake on the police car that blocks the gang's escape, he is followed by Blanche, running along in blind panic. As the gang bursts from the garage in its car, pushes the police car out of the way, and bypasses the road block in the street, we also see Blanche running along the other corner of the screen. The gang has been welded into a professional unit by their daring escape, but Blanche's hysterical terror, though almost frighteningly funny, is also a sign of the human cost of the choice the gang has made and a foreshadowing of their ultimate fate.

6. *The Taunting of Frank Hamer*

There are two fundamental consequences of the Joplin gun battle and escape: the gang is now completely committed to the role of bandits, and there is no longer any chance of escape from the consequences of their criminal actions, for they have killed not only citizens but policemen. In this episode, both these aspects of the gang's situation are dramatized. With the appearance of Frank Hamer, we see that the Barrows have encountered a nemesis, a figure so implacable in his determination to capture or destroy the gang that his approach is like the onset of doom. Hamer's implacability is effectively represented in the scene by his size and immovability. Although he is quickly captured by the gang, he remains silent and impenetrable in the midst of the horseplay and violence of the gang. In our last view of him, he is seated in a small boat in the midst of a pond, glaring fatefully after the gang, and we realize that Bonnie and Clyde have left behind an opponent they can never escape.

Some viewers have objected to the one-dimensional portrait of Hamer as an almost villainous picture of the dehumanized manhunter. In appearance and manner, he is clearly intended to suggest the mythical figure of the Western sheriff. Indeed, the scene begins with a Western-style shoot-out in which Clyde shoots the gun out of Hamer's hand in good Lone Ranger fashion. However, although Hamer certainly is a stock figure in many ways, this is appropriate to his function in the action as the fateful pursuer. If he had more complex characteristics, if, for example, the film tried to explore his personal background and suggest complex motives for his implacable hatred of Bonnie and Clyde, the focus of the action would inevitably shift somewhat from the rise and fall of Bonnie and Clyde to the purposes of their pursuers. The earlier version of the script actually suggests a much more complex view of the character in the following interplay with Bonnie:

Suddenly, we see that she begins purposefully touching him in a highly sexually charged manner. She continues this, smiling into his eyes.

Close-up Hamer. As Bonnie continues taunting him, he begins to crack. His face reveals a furious battle going on inside him. Bonnie's maneuver and presence is unceasing, insistent. Hamer's façade cracks: his lips twitch, his eyes blink, and harden. She has reached him and unmanned him at last.

Hamer: (with frightening intensity) Take your hands off me.

In the shooting script and in the film, the complex sexual implications of the scene are completely eliminated:

She (Bonnie) coyly loosens his tie, tousles his hair, and plants a big kiss on him while still ogling camera.

Moreover, in the original script, Clyde's violent attack on Hamer was motivated in large part by his jealousy of Bonnie's explicitly sexual play. In the film, Clyde's outburst, solely the result of his anger at Hamer's role as pursuer, is intensified by Hamer's spitting at Bonnie.

Because of this one-dimensional treatment, Hamer remains a symbolic figure, and we are inclined to see the scene in symbolic terms: as the gang encountering its nemesis and struggling fruitlessly to overcome it. Neither antics and horseplay nor outright violence makes an impact on Hamer's contemptuous and brutal composure. And this sequence of actions, from the comic shoot-out and the jibes with the camera, to the outburst of violence in which Clyde attacks the handcuffed Hamer and then finally sets him adrift in a small boat, is a microcosm of the development of the film from comic horseplay to destructive violence.

This episode also shows the gang becoming increasingly immersed in its role as heroic bandits. At the beginning of the scene, the group has grabbed a newspaper from a rural mailbox and is eagerly devouring the legend of their exploits. So immersed are they in the newspaper story that they do not notice Hamer's approach. But Clyde has gone off into the woods to relieve himself and is therefore able to surprise Hamer from behind. His Western-style shootdown with Hamer is another expression of the increasing dominance of legendary role over human personality. Finally, when the gang handcuffs Hamer and takes his picture among them, they express a faith in the image, as if taking Hamer's photo with the gang could somehow negate his power against them. There are also disturbing undercurrents in the scene, reflecting the escalating violence that has been unleashed between the gang and the law, and the realization that the bandits' role must inevitably lead to death. Clyde really wants to kill Hamer and he is twice dissuaded from further violence by Buck and Bonnie. In short, this episode is an effective representation of the gang's transformation into professional outlaws trapped in their own legend. They are still capable of horseplay and funning around, but the play has come to seem a fragile façade through which violence continually threatens to break. The gang has become a legend, but they have also met and failed to break the power of the force that will destroy them. Even Clyde's attempt to justify himself by appealing to the social injustice of the law is immediately undercut by his own unrestrained attack on the handcuffed Hamer when the latter spits on Bonnie.

7. The Third Bank Robbery

The representation of this robbery shows the gang at the height of its powers and is the supreme embodiment of the Barrow legend. The tone is once again one of almost farcical comedy, as in some of the opening episodes. This is a fine artistic stroke at this point, for we have the powerful irony of seeing the gang at the peak of its success and yet knowing that they are running, out of control, toward their destruction. Unlike the previous robberies, everything goes off without a mistake, the gang functioning with smooth teamwork and pride in their role. Clyde begins the robbery by announcing almost like a radio program, "Good afternoon, this is the Barrow gang." From that point on everybody plays his part—the old farmer is allowed to keep his money, a harmless shot reduces the guard to impotence, Buck proudly announces his name as he takes a pair of sunglasses from the guard to give to Blanche for a birthday present —and in a farcical chase the gang escapes across the state line, followed by the policeman's comic tag "I ain't goin' to risk my life in Oklahoma." To carry out the motif of the individual swallowed up in the legend, the scene is intercut with reactions by people at the scene of the crime in which we can already see the elaboration of the legend. The chase is exuberant, the intercutting helps build up a sense of comic suspense and final release, and for a moment it seems as if the spontaneous gaiety of the film's opening has been restored. Yet one realizes that the old farmer has the last word in the way he recognizes the inevitable fatality that has been set in motion: "and all's I can say is, they did right by me, and I'm bringin' me a mess of flowers to their funeral." And the balloon is finally punctured when, after their successful escape, the gang stops along the road to split their take. It is pitifully small and they bicker over the division, showing that the exciting public legend can neither support them nor contain their personal needs and conflicts.

8. The Gun Battle at the Platte City Motel

Two episodes occur between the third bank robbery and the Platte City gunfight: the kidnapping of the undertaker Eugene Grizzard and his girlfriend, Velma, and the family picnic at which Bonnie says goodbye to her mother. Both these scenes represent attempts by the gang to reestablish some kind of connection with ordinary, normal life, and both end in ominous recognitions of the inevitable destruction awaiting them. The wild ride with Eugene and his girlfriend is a moment of strained hilarity. The gang, isolated in its car and lonely for human companionship, desperately tries to make friends and enjoy a moment of ordinary social intercourse. There is considerable humor in the incongruity of the now legendary Barrow gang trying to act just "like folks" and in the terrified reaction of Eugene and Velma turning to a kind of hysterical release when they finally realize that they are not going to be murdered. But the strain remains. One is never quite sure that latent violence will not erupt again in some irrational way. Finally, when Eugene reveals that he is an undertaker, there is a moment of terrible silence until we see that Bonnie accepts the omen of death without reacting violently, only insisting that Eugene and Velma be put out of the car immediately.

The family picnic is another attempt to restore some contact with life. Penn films it in soft focus and opens the episode with a dream-like montage of picnic scenes to suggest the futility of Bonnie's hope of reentering her past and finding solace in the arms of her mother. The scene ends with dark foreshadowing when Mrs. Barrow punctures Clyde's fantasy of settling down with the simple devastating remark:

You try to live three miles from me and you won't live long,
honey. You'd best keep runnin' and you know it, Clyde Barrow.

Against this immediate background, the Platte City episode begins. Unlike the Joplin gunfight, the gang escapes from this battle
with Buck and Blanche badly wounded only to face another even
more desperate fight in the strange light of dawn. The filming of
the Platte City battle brings out the theme of escalating violence,
which, generated by Clyde's initial gunshot in the opening episode,
mounts in scale until the initiative passes from Bonnie and Clyde
to their pursuers and the gang is swallowed up in the maelstrom of
death they have unknowingly and unintentionally set off. The
Joplin gunfight was filmed in daylight and edited in such a way as
to emphasize the confusion of isolated individual actions until the
gang finally seized the initiative and escaped. In Platte City, the
effect is of two opposing forces firing and tearing at each other in
mindless abandon. Filmed at night, the scene is focussed around a
long shot showing the forces of the law with their armored car on
one side and the beleaguered motel on the other. A moving searchlight illuminates only portions of the scene; the rest we see dimly,
in the glare of gunfire and the explosion of hand grenades. The
cutting moves in almost the opposite direction from that of the
Joplin sequence. Here, the actions of the gang, desperately trying
to escape, become increasingly fragmented and confused, their movements lit fitfully by the blinding glare of searchlight and explosives.
By the end of the scene, they are all screaming and shouting in contrast to the single panicky hysteria of Blanche in the Joplin affair.
Although they do finally escape, there is only a momentary respite
before the firing begins again in the next episode.

9. The Battle at Dexter, Iowa

This is the end for the gang. After this battle, only C. W. escapes
without being seriously wounded, while Buck is killed and Blanche
captured. The battle is filmed in such a way as to emphasize the
isolation and helplessness of Bonnie and Clyde against the overpowering force gathered against them and to show how their aggression against society has given rise to a reaction equally uncontrolled
in its violence. The initiative in action has clearly passed over from
criminals to pursuers in the battle of the night before. As the scene

begins, the gang is resting in a field, torn and bloody, with Buck mortally wounded. Dawn comes up, soft and beautiful, the light on the trees reminiscent of earlier images of trees that formed the background for the beginning of Bonnie and Clyde's romance. But, with the coming of the light, it is apparent that the trees are full of armed men and that the gang is hopelessly surrounded. The gang staggers into its car and moves around the circle of the trees seeking an escape. An extreme long shot of the scene makes it clear that they are trapped in a ring of fire. In general, this scene is shot in medium long and long shot, and the action is given an almost surrealistic, nightmarish quality consonant with the total entrapment of the gang. For the first time, Bonnie and Clyde cannot make their escape by car. The car in which they hopelessly circle the interior of the ring of fire is hung up on a stump, and their second car is demolished by concentrated gunfire before they can get to it. This destruction of the gang's cars becomes the focal point of this battle. It expresses both the irrational rage for destruction of the pursuing posse and the extent to which the mythical power of the gang has been based on their identification with the car. Separated from their car, Bonnie and Clyde become vulnerable and are both seriously wounded in the battle. Though they finally escape on foot, and C. W. manages to steal another car to drive them away, the nature of their lives and power has undergone a final transformation. From this point, they become figures in a ritual of suffering and death, their own powers of initiative and aggression having finally yielded to the overwhelming force of the pursuit. This change is finally expressed in the scene of the Okie camp that follows immediately after the escape from the Dexter battle. As the Okies gather around the wounded Bonnie and Clyde, slumped bleeding and barely conscious in the back seat of the car, there is a reverential awe on their watching faces and in the actions of those who reach in to touch the battered figures. The ceremonial quality of this scene clearly suggests the recognition not simply of the legend of Bonnie and Clyde's super power, but also the feeling of fatality and sacrifice.

10. The Final Ambush

The handling of the final ambush posed a difficult artistic problem for Penn and his co-workers. The story called for the most brutal and violent destruction of the protagonists. This was not only the

fate of the historical Bonnie and Clyde, but the classic ending of
the gangster picture; the protagonist, having overreached himself,
is gunned down either by the law or by fellow gangsters. In addition,
the mounting crescendo of violence that marks the development of
Bonnie and Clyde clearly required some climactic act of slaughter
to carry through the theme of battle and pursuit generated by the
series of gun battles we have just analyzed. Yet, if this scene had to
be an apogee of violence, it also had to carry with it some resolu-
tion of the drama and some sense of what the audience is to make of
it. How could the scene be filmed in such a way as to bring the
presentation of violence to its extreme point and yet to bring the
action to a point beyond sheer chaos, to make the audience respond
to the final tragedy of Bonnie and Clyde and to reach some understanding of what this tragedy means?

The tragedy of Bonnie and Clyde can perhaps best be summed
up as the story of two people who sought meaningful human goals
—love, personal loyalty, individual dignity, the transcendence of
constricting and diminishing social roles—in such a distorted way as
to make these goals impossible of attainment. Instead, their mistaken
choice of a means to these ends led to an inevitable and terrible
fall, because, by resorting to violence, they released a complex social
force that inevitably had to track them down and destroy them. The
special power of the ending of *Bonnie and Clyde* lies not only in the
way it makes us feel the terrible culminating violence of the action,
but in its expression of the final recognition that Bonnie and Clyde
have about each other, and in its development of the theme of
ritual sacrifice to society's own impulses toward violence.

The episodes leading up to the final scene interrelate the idyllic
culmination of the relationship between Bonnie and Clyde with
their betrayal by C. W.'s father. The sexual fulfillment of the romance between the two protagonists is tragically ironic because, as
we see from the inevitable betrayal, Bonnie and Clyde have en-
meshed themselves in the net of crime and retribution too deeply to
be able to disengage. Moreover, Clyde doesn't really want to anyway.
Yet the fact that the couple have been able to express their need for
transcendence sexually, instead of through crime, restores to them
some of their earlier charm and innocence, and makes their death
seem particularly terrible, though inevitable. To emphasize this
quality of the two protagonists as they approach their death, Bonnie
is dressed in white, and before they leave to drive into the ambush,

she shows Clyde a tiny figurine of a shepherdess she has purchased, a figure both symbolic of the pastoral idyll they have been attempting on the Moss farm and reminiscent of the decor of Bonnie's room in the opening sequence. Clyde has taken off his shoes and loses one lens from his sunglasses. These latter are rather effective symbols. On the surface, they typify Clyde's impulsive spontaneity and sense of fun: why not drive with one's shoes off if that's more comfortable? and as to the sunglasses, one can always drive with one eye shut. But these symbols have more ominous overtones. The shoes remind us of Buck's dying words, "I believe I lost my shoes . . . maybe the dog hid 'em," and the sunglasses remind us of Blanche's wounded eyes, for she was wearing the sunglasses Buck gave her when they were surrounded at Platte City. In addition, these particular symbols have larger conventional associations: glasses with blindness and sight, ignorance and knowledge; and shoes with society and its roles and norms. Finally, as they drive toward the ambush, this sequence of symbolic gestures culminates in Bonnie offering Clyde a piece of fruit. With its reference back to the Edenic overtones of the opening sequence and its complex reminder of the life and death the two have offered each other, this final gesture symbolically rounds out the circle Bonnie and Clyde have followed and prepares us for the final tragedy.

Benton and Newman's original conception of the final scene is interestingly different from the scene as it was finally shot; yet their work did establish a basic conception of the scene that was developed and changed in the process of shooting and editing. In the following description, we can see the writers grappling with the problem of representing a peak of violence as well as giving a tragic meaning and expression to the deaths of the protagonists:

> The gunfight takes just seconds during which the law fires eighty-seven shots at Bonnie and Clyde, giving them absolutely no chance. The SOUND is rapid, deafening.
>
> *At no point* in the gun fight do we see Bonnie and Clyde in motion. We see, instead, two still photographs CUT INTO the sequence: one of Clyde, half out of the car, taking careful dead aim with his gun, just as he did in the teaching scene; one of Bonnie in terror, pack of cigarettes in her hand clutched tight, looking as fragile and beautiful as she can be.
>
> The NOISE stops at once. Utter silence. It has been a massacre. Bonnie and Clyde never had a chance to return the gunfire. We

see the car, a complete shambles. We never see Bonnie and Clyde dead, though for a moment we discern their bodies slumped in the car.

This conception would probably have been fairly effective as it stands.

Penn, however, evidently felt that the action in *Bonnie and Clyde* develops to such an intense and tragic level that the ending must wring out the audience emotionally in a way that the more static earlier conception would not. Still, the basic idea of manipulating the motion of the protagonists stayed with the sequence, transformed into a combination of stop action and slow motion that is strikingly powerful.

The ambush is another of those intricately edited sequences composed of an extraordinary number of short individual cuts that characterize most of the key scenes in the film. In general, the sequence can be divided into four main parts. In the first, Bonnie and Clyde's car is waved down by C. W. Moss's father, whose truck is parked by the side of the road with a faked flat tire. This scene is done in alternating close shots of the three main characters, interrupted by a long shot of an approaching truck, which will force the hidden posse to shoot before the truck shields the two criminals. The second part of the sequence begins with a middle shot of the bushes behind which the posse is hidden. The cause for this shot is a sudden flight of birds that startles Bonnie and Clyde and quickly makes them realize that something is wrong. An extraordinary series of rapidly alternating close shots of Bonnie and Clyde work toward a crescendo of extreme close shots, in which we see the following sequence of reactions: the suddenly perplexed feeling that something is wrong; then, the sense that an ambush is present; and finally, in a brief series of extreme close shots that have the feeling of stopped action, the two look at each other with love and a kind of ultimate recognition and acceptance of their mutual destruction. In particular, a strikingly posed shot of Bonnie carries a complex feeling of affirmation of all that Clyde has meant to her. This part of the sequence achieves a powerful expressiveness by the combination of the quickness of the cuts and the static character of the action. We sense a fixed moment in time, as if the two characters would like to prolong their last glance at each other forever. And then, the storm breaks, marked again by a shot of those ominous bushes, this time

1. Warren Beatty as Clyde Barrow, Faye Dunaway as Bonnie Parker. All photos from The Museum of Modern Art/Film Stills Archive.

2. Bonnie and Clyde rob their first grocery store. Clyde is
attacked by the butcher, whom he shoots.

3. Bonnie tries to make love to Clyde, forcing him to reveal his impotence.

4. The gun battle at Joplin.

5. Bonnie during the high point of the gang's bank-robbing career.

6. C. W. Moss (Michael J. Pollard), Buck Barrow (Gene Hackman), and Bonnie and Clyde make their getaway.

7. C. W. Moss shoots it out with police at the Platte City Motel.

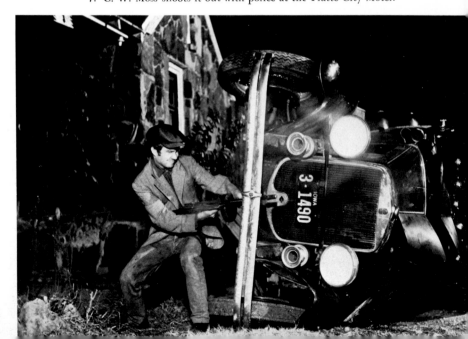

8. Blanche Barrow (Estelle Parsons) is captured and Buck Barrow is killed during the battle with police at Dexter, Iowa.

9. C. W. and Bonnie and Clyde escape.

10. The three remaining members of the gang are attacked while crossing a river.

11. C. W. and Clyde with the seriously wounded Bonnie.

breaking out in a hail of gunfire. The third part of the sequence has perhaps the most striking and haunting image of the entire film, the picture of Bonnie's body writhing in slow motion as it is penetrated by bullet after bullet. This, together with the similar treatment of Clyde as he rolls along the ground buffeted by the impact of the posse's guns, becomes a final and terrible orgy of violence, qualified only by the camera's gradual movement back out of the action, from medium to long shot.

The slow-motion agony of Bonnie and Clyde has an almost unbearable intensity of feeling that the original conception of still photographs does not. In this way, the sequence insures the strongest possible emotional response to the destruction of the tragic protagonists. Because of the sexual character of Bonnie's final death throes, emphasized by the slow motion treatment, the scene becomes a terrible, ironic perversion of the sexual act. Bonnie and Clyde find an ultimate orgasm in their destruction, which turns out to be the final goal of their desperate strivings for fulfillment. And to remind us of the basic perversion of love that led to the tragedy, the impact of the guns, while bringing on this horrible parody of sexual ecstasy, actually drive them farther apart. Only when the guns stop do the two move desperately and futilely toward each other in the final slump of death.

This treatment of the protagonists' deaths also expresses another important theme. Just as the writhings of Bonnie and Clyde sum up the problem of the ambiguous relationship between love and violence in their relationship, so do they call attention to the perverse and complex nature of the relationship between Bonnie and Clyde and their destroyers. It is the gunshots of the posse that cause this horrifying violation of the body with its grotesque parody of sexual ecstasy. Thus, the scene seems like a rape, with all its connotations of pleasure in violation, rather than an execution, an act of reluctant and painful duty. Such a representation symbolizes in visual terms the concept of the perverse relationship between the criminal and those who hunt him down that is developed in the film. In a number of ways throughout the film, such as the escalating violence of the pursuers and the increasing importance of the social legend of Bonnie and Clyde, we see how the protagonists' crimes become objects of fascination to society and finally justifications for acts of violence more deliberate and brutal than the criminal acts that generated them. Thus, between criminal and society grows up a complex and perverse relationship in which collective urges toward anarchy and violence find expression through the punishment of crime.

From this point of view, the criminal's destruction can be seen as a kind of victimization and ritual sacrifice to a social tension between repulsion and attraction to violence. To bear this out, the film plays ironically with the audience's fascination with the figure of the gangster, an interest reflecting the kind of ambiguous collective feelings that the society represented in the film expresses by both glorifying and destroying Bonnie and Clyde. The final orgy of violence is profoundly disturbing precisely because it is a prolongation, through slow motion, of the horrible and the fascinating, of terrible pain and perverse sexual excitement. Thus, this part of the final sequence brings together in a single image the complex relation to violence of protagonists, antagonists, and audience that lies at the heart of the film.

The fourth and final section of the ambush sequence is also the end of the film. It represents the posse, the betrayer, and the innocent bystanders from the passing truck gathering around the car. In awesome silence, a tracking shot passes over the car and then, in a shot through the bullet-riddled car windows, shows the men gathered around. Then, the film blacks out. The effect of this brief section suggests a complex feeling of awe and wonder at what has been done. It is a visual analogue to the choric comment that typically ends tragedies. A terrible quiet ensues which still seems to echo with the sound of gunfire. We leave the world of the film with a haunting awareness of the tragic things men can do to each other.

BONNIE AND CLYDE
by CHARLES THOMAS SAMUELS

A bunch of decayed cabbage leaves smeared with catsup, *Bonnie and Clyde* has been judged an artistic bouquet; not by middlebrow critics like Bosley Crowther but by reviewers whose very names stand for the setting and guiding of taste. Admittedly, the film is well-acted, slickly paced, and brilliantly edited. Yet after granting its technical polish, one is left with its meaning, which is heavily obvious when not confused; its tone and characterization, which are both implausible and inconsistent; and its violence, which is stomach-turning. One who measures its cynical falsity will realize how worrisome is its success.

To begin with, *Bonnie and Clyde* is presumed to be making serious comments about crime. So far as I can see, the comments are these: crime is joyless, it is sick, it is less concerned with money than fame. As an example of the first point, we have the scene at a motel in which Clyde's brother hoots and hollers, "Whooee, we'll have ourselves a time."—Long pause—"What we gonna do?"—followed by Clyde's account of how he avoided prison work by cutting off two toes, concluded with a broad smile and an "Ain't life grand!" To establish the bankrobber's sickness, we have at least four instances of Clyde's impotence that presumably explain his reliance on more lethal weapons. By way of asserting that the criminals seek publicity rather than gain, we have the Barrows stealing a newspaper from a rural mailbox before they count the proceeds from their latest bank. It is difficult to understand how insights so dramatized can be taken seriously; but Joseph Morgenstern, who on first viewing thought *Bonnie and Clyde* "a squalid shoot-'em-up for the

From The Hudson Review *21, no. 1 (Spring 1968): 10–22. Reprinted by permission of the author.*

moron trade," acknowledged great purposiveness and subtlety when *Newsweek* permitted him a public reversal the following week.

Viewers might well find themselves confused, for the film shuttles back and forth between radically different tones. Through most of the gang's activities, fast pacing and banjo music contrive to turn mayhem into zaniness and the bloody Barrows into charming hicks; but, in addition to being primitive, these scenes violate characterization and plausibility. Take, for example, Clyde's first bank robbery. As Bonnie drives him to the site of the crime, he seems as nervous as a raw recruit, yet we know that he has already served time for what he here contemplates with dread. (One might argue that this shows Clyde to be a frightened punk, but usually, as in the woods or the café before this job, he is made to seem authoritative, even sensitive.) When Bonnie finally shames him into action, he discovers that the bank is out of business. Considerately, the management has left a teller behind to inform him of the fact; but, of course, without the teller, there would be no comedy. Even more absurd is their second job, during which the get-away man, C. W. Moss, nearly ruins everything by backing into a parking place— guided less by his own stupidity than by the scriptwriters' desire for laughs. Eventually Moss pulls out, but his delay permits the bank's employees to chase him. Here the film turns suddenly gory, a fact that has occasioned its admirers' most sophistical argument.

Pauline Kael asserts that the comedy purposefully turns into violence in order to implicate the viewer, who will be harrowed when he realizes that crime isn't, after all, fun: "the whole point of *Bonnie and Clyde* is to rub our noses in it, to make us pay our dues for laughing." What Miss Kael neglects to admit is that we laugh only because the director and writers have forced us—by wrenching their materials to fit a comic mold. Penelope Gilliatt recognizes that "the movie is full of scenes of giggling and show-off, but the mood belongs to the characters, not the film." One would be interested to see how she might go about arguing this distinction.

When sexually motivating the protagonists' crimes—that is to say, when introducing psychology to tone matters up—the film becomes not only implausible but dishonest. Scenarists David Newman and Robert Benton have recently confessed that Clyde was originally to have been homosexual rather than impotent, "but we [made the change] because homosexuality took over the whole movie and colored all responses." Translated less ingenuously, this comes out:

whereas homosexuality repels the average spectator, impotence is likely to make him sympathetic. After all, Clyde is a hero.

Similarly motivated are the many hints that Bonnie and Clyde were heroes because America was undergoing a Depression. This note is first struck when Clyde invites a dispossessed farmer to shoot the sign placed before his house by the bank. Throughout the film, its director and set designer take great trouble duplicating the thirties in order to surround the Barrows with an ambience of social decay so palpable that mere presence might suggest causality. Thus we are disposed to believe Clyde when he promises Bonnie's mother that they will stop stealing as soon as times improve, and we can sympathize when the couple is forced to steal food because the bank they had previously attempted had already failed. But apart from the offensive facility with which it yokes public circumstance and private crime, occasionally the film argues against its own implication. Before they are killed, for example, when Bonnie asks Clyde what he would do with his life to live over, after an intense moment of concentration, he replies that he would pull his jobs in other states.

Bonnie and Clyde runs off in many directions at once (even Pauline Kael, who runs off in quite a few herself, calls it at one point, "the first film demonstration that the put-on can be used for the purposes of art"). Yet though all of its admirers are aware that the film might be called wayward, they either de-emphasize or ignore its banal confusion. But since *Bonnie and Clyde* is so confused, its violence shows all the more lurid against the vague thematic background. The interesting questions to raise about the film therefore are why so many reputable critics condone violence lacking expressive purpose and why customers are willing to pay for a movie both repulsive in its bloodshed and disorienting in its tonal shifts. What holds the film together for these groups who themselves form so unexpected a combination?

We can approach an answer by way of the movie's most discussed episode. When Bonnie returns to her mother, the director shoots the scene in soft focus, emphasizing not only the dusty atmosphere in which it transpires but the haze of nostalgia and family feeling through which its participants perceive themselves. Bonnie's family is delighted to welcome the returning prodigals; they have kept a scrapbook of the gang's exploits. Bonnie romps with the children; Clyde, the good son-in-law, enjoys the vittles. We might be witness-

ing the family picnic of all our dreams—until Bonnie's mother tells
her daughter and Clyde to keep on running from the cops. This
ironic reversal, however, is too pat and unsurprising to dissipate the
foregoing effect of lyricism, especially since the picnic is preceded by
another scene of lyricism so fruity that we are now thoroughly confused. In the earlier scene, Clyde pursues Bonnie as she flees the
gang to make her way home. Catching up with her in a golden wheat-
field, he wails plaintively, "Please don't never leave me without
sayin' nuttin." Accompanied by soulful music, the loving couple
embraces, while the camera draws back, leaving them a poor tangled
speck in a giant sea of grain over which portentous clouds glide,
casting shadows. Under the circumstances, this might seem a sick
joke: casting the crooks—previously clowns or desperadoes—in the
roles of Mr. Newlywed and the young wife who wants to run home
to mother. But like several other scenes, it creates unmistakable
identification between the Barrows and the audience; and it is this
identification which holds the spectator. Then, having persuaded
the audience to identify with the Barrows, the film goes on to suggest
that the crooks are superior to society. Here the serious critics seem
to have found their delight.

It may seem tedious to recall the many ways in which the film
slanders society, but I don't think one can understand its current
popularity until this motif has been explored. Its presentation is
relentless, beginning when the hungry but penniless Clyde attempts
to steal groceries. While he inquires after peach pie, a piggish clerk
flies down at him with a meat cleaver, thus nearly validating his
subsequent chagrin: "He tried to kill me. I didn't wanna hurt him.
You try to get somep'n to eat round here, they come at you with a
meat cleaver." Throughout the film, the forces of property and law
respond with excessive, even sadistic zeal. Not only do they require
1000 rounds of ammunition to finish the lovers off but when the
gang tries to settle down in tidy domesticity, the cops intrude without even the chivalrous warning one has come to expect from
earlier gangster movies ("All right, come out now; the house is
surrounded!"). Ambushing the Barrows at a motel, the police un-
fairly arrive in an armored car at just the moment when Bonnie is
showing Clyde how she has taken in an old dress; and when they
kill Clyde's brother by surrounding him as he's down, the deputies
shout like Comanche savages, in whose classic formation they have

been staged. Yet though the besieged gang kills its share, the law-men, unlike the criminals, never bleed.

If we turn our attention to the Barrows' only differentiated antagonists, the film's bias becomes unmistakable. The sheriff who finally kills the lovers sports a devilish mustache and, in the death scene, wears a black shirt, though everything about Bonnie and Clyde, including their car, is white. Critics have admired the film's insight into the crooks' pathetic desire for publicity. Sheriff Hamer is similarly motivated, but in his case the impulse is bad: he goes after Bonnie and Clyde out of vengeance, because they humiliated him by circulating the photo in which they forced him to pose as their captive.

Because the gang's antagonists are pigs and devils who wear black shirts and don't bleed, and because they have formed a society actually inferior to that of the criminals,[1] in which brotherhood and love predominate, we can sympathize with the Barrows, even though they are hard to keep in rational focus. But because the criminals are sick, dumb, and ludicrous, we can bear to watch them die. Citing this latter characteristic, Pauline Kael argues that *Bonnie and Clyde* is less sentimental than standard Hollywood gangster films because they used to make the criminals innocent. But in drama, if not in life, innocence is relative. The movie clearly authorizes Bonnie's doggerel characterization of herself and Clyde as scapegoats whom society will not leave in peace.

Thereby forced into partisanship, a spectator can actually ap-prove the blood as the red badge of Bonnie and Clyde's undeserved suffering. Critics, of course, have found something deeper in it. More or less overt in every favorable review is the notion that *Bonnie and Clyde* makes a valid comment not so much on their lives as on ours. We know better than the thirties that violence may substitute for love, that it is often perpetrated by moral morons, that America

---

[1] At no time is the film's comedy more heavily thematic than when the gang kidnaps the couple, Eugene and Velma. By turns, we are treated to exposures of the couple's prurience, cowardice, and secret regard for crime. Though blatant, all this has some relevance. Why though, do we get the revelation that Velma has lied to Eugene about her age? For the same reason that the respectable Mr. Moss, who will betray Bonnie and Clyde, shouts at his son, "I'm glad that your ma ain't alive to see this thing," meaning not C. W.'s crime but his tattoo. And for the same reason that the one member of the gang who is disloyal, dishonest, and greedy is Blanche—the preacher's daughter.

today incites violence by its disrespect for law and people. "All this should strike the viewer with icy familiarity," asserts Robert Hatch (an editor of *The Nation*) "in our day of motorcycle gangs and flower children, Nazi insignia, cheap beads, incense, drugs, apathy and motiveless violence." Whereas the audience probably identifies with Bonnie and Clyde as surrogate social victims, serious reviewers identify them as surrogate social problems. No wonder, despite the bloodshed, that everyone is happy.

But the movie's inventors give a less edifying account of their product's appeal: violence in the arts, they say, is "fun," "and if that idea causes you to blanch or cluck the tongue reprovingly . . . then you are not only soft . . . you are something worse: out of step." As Pauline Kael reports with equanimity, "in the spoofs of the last few years, everything is gross, ridiculous, insane; to make sense would be to risk being square."

Ironically, whereas Newman and Benton (creators of *Esquire's* "What's In and What's Out" and Dubious Achievement Awards) think violence fun and significance a drag, reviewers and moviegoers have, through their earnest pursuit of the movie's purpose, turned *Bonnie and Clyde* into the year's most successful and—the ads bray—"most talked-about film." This irony is the true key to the film's meaning, for as *Newsweek* reports, Newman and Benton "always seem to know what's going to pop up next in American culture."

Lurid example of a vulgar, wornout genre, *Bonnie and Clyde* nevertheless seems up-to-date. Not because of its technique, out of Godard and the vaudeville blackout; not because of its ideas, out of *Sanctuary* (the impotent gunman) or Erik Erikson (the identity crisis), but because of an attitude which persuades the viewer to swallow its violence: the attitude—it is precisely nothing more—that society and normality are frauds. Since this is close to having become a contemporary article of faith, it is no wonder that violence has become as entertaining in art as it seems to have become excusable in politics. Oppose the latter, and you are a soft-hearted liberal; oppose the former, and you are "something worse: out of step."

That Bosley Crowther is "out of step" should come as no surprise. When for once, however, he marched slowly in a good cause, he brought down upon his head anger so fierce that we can now see how precious a possession the film's attitude has become. Thus Penelope Gilliat, obviously thinking of Crowther, said that one would need "a head full of wooden shavings" to think that the movie glamorized crime, though if the word "glamorize" is correctly understood it is entirely to the point. Thus Pauline Kael, obviously thinking of Crowther, begins her piece in a manner uniquely wistful: "How do you make a good movie in this country without being jumped on?" (Miss Kael, it should be explained, thinks *"Bonnie and Clyde . . .* the most excitingly American American movie since *The Manchurian Candidate!"* Thus Andrew Sarris felt called upon to begin his review in *The Village Voice* by informing readers that *"Bonnie and Clyde* has become the subject of a Crowther crusade that makes the 100-Years-War look like a border incident" (a remark whose inaptness would inspire hyperbole had Sarris not already pre-empted the heights). In fact, so enraged is Sarris that he charges poor Crowther with a crime of which Crowther was manifestly innocent: calling for censorship, "at a time when too many bigots see a golden opportunity to lash the Negro with fake rhetoric of law and order."

Sarris' absurd political analogy suggests the covertly political basis of most of the film's support, a phenomenon even more strikingly displayed by the irate letter-writers who bombarded the *Times* after Crowther's review appeared. But at the same time that the film's attitude suggests affinities with some current political notions, its supporters don't want it taken too seriously. One almost hears them tremble: if the establishment really sees what is going on in *Bonnie and Clyde* they may spoil the fun by taking it away from us! Thus, after coming to realize that its use of violence was relevant, Joseph Morgenstern spins about to assert that "when we talk about movies, even artistic movies, we are not talking about urban-renewal programs, nuclear non-proliferation treaties or rat-control bills." Yet Morgenstern then goes on to argue that the film's violence takes its significance from the fact that "most of humanity teeters on the edge of violence every day."

Does *Bonnie and Clyde* have political or social significance far beyond its significance as a work of art? To answer "yes" is not to contend that the film incites acts directly, for against such a contention Morgenstern would be right and Sarris would have reason to fear thought control. But art initiates action in more subtle ways:

by reflecting contemporary attitudes and thus, through the power of reflection, confirming them. How much more potent is this process when performed by a piece of mass entertainment.

It would be foolish to equate the growing approval of violence, even among humane and liberal persons, with the specific advocacy of a bloodthirsty, cheap film. Those who riot against conditions in the Negro ghetto or the war in Vietnam can claim precisely the moral validation for their acts which the Barrow Gang so conspicuously lacks. But each form of behavior embodies a similar lapse of commitment to organized society, and in accepting one we may find ourselves accepting the other. Each expresses the underlying belief that society represents not law and order but only convention and force. When society is no longer felt to represent legitimacy, protest itself becomes the only legitimate response. But with standards of legitimacy confounded, the criminal may seem to resemble the rebel, the hippie to merge with the reformer. Surely *Bonnie and Clyde* did not produce society's current disrepute or our desperate reaching out for any alternative. Just as surely, by playing with the disrepute it exploits the desperation, helping us to celebrate what we once condemned.

If seeing the film as a reflection of larger social issues seems far-fetched, I commend the reader's attention to an important study of the German expressionist film after World War I: Siegfried Kracauer's *From Caligari to Hitler* (Princeton, 1947; reissued, 1966). Assuming that movies are an index to national mentality because they are collectively produced and massively consumed, Kracauer traces through the period's chief films the rise of Nazism. In short, he implies that popular entertainment acts as a national fever chart. In the thirties in Germany, the disease was authoritarianism; in the sixties in America, it is anarchy. Through the stream of anarchic art which flows high and low in our culture today, *Bonnie and Clyde* thrashes prominently, its protagonists folk heroes in a national epic struggle.

The day after I saw the film, at the school where I teach—a very good school with intelligent students from comfortable homes—I saw scrawled on a bathroom wall, "C. W. in '68." If this example of collegiate graffiti is portentous to even a small degree, then investigating the importance of *Bonnie and Clyde* can't be left to reviewers.

BONNIE AND CLYDE:
Society vs. the Clan
by CAROLYN GEDULD

Of the many recent films which have bridged the gap between art and popular appeal, Arthur Penn's *Bonnie and Clyde* has probably been the most controversial. The film has been attacked for the wrong reasons, as, for example, by critics who object to its association of crime and "fun"; while among those more concerned with aesthetics than sociology, it has been interpreted as a Hollywood response to the French "take over" of American genres. Essentially, to such critics, *Bonnie and Clyde* seems to be a Truffaut-Godard type parody of the gangster film. However, a better case might be made for it as a parody of the Western. But the impact of the film is to be found not so much in its elements of parody as in its dramatic shifts of mood between parody and horror. There is a clinical fascination with shots of flesh being shattered by bullets, which is heightened by the comic sequences preceding them—a use of dramatic contrast seen before in *Italiano Bravo Gente*. If the violent episodes are not a sort of gimmick inserted into lighter sequences merely to "shake" the audience, they must be justified in terms of the film's larger interests.

Basically, the ambivalence of the film originates in a narrative which combines domestic comedy with the "Jesse James" style of Western. In the mood of the former, the emphasis is on Bonnie and Clyde as "plain folk" who tell bad jokes, have religious affiliations, sexual problems, and family reunions, and who are, we are constantly reminded, "just like us." In the mood of the Western, by con-

From Film Heritage *3, no. 2 (Winter 1967–68). Reprinted by permission of the author.*

trast, they are "different," a breed apart from the domestic involvements of society: the Barrow gang who rob banks, kill, escape in stagecoach-cars, rest in motel hideouts, and are eventually ambushed and shot by the "posse." The two genres are, of course, antithetical. Traditionally, the domestic comedy suggests that no matter what insanity abounds, the family unit will prevail. In the *Blondie* series, for instance, despite the threat of chaos and anarchy, the structure of the household cannot be destroyed and domestic values remain intact. In the "Jesse James" type of Western, on the other hand, domestic values are subverted or upset, and consequently, anything goes. The nomadic life itself inimical to permanence, and typically, the gang-on-the-run is destroyed by internal dissension: the unfaithful moll, the argument about division of the spoils, the struggle for power, the "squealer." Often the gang begins to dissolve when members are killed by their colleagues, long before the final ambush.

When, in *Bonnie and Clyde*, domestic comedy and the Western meet head on, rather like a mixture of *The Family Way* and *The Dalton Brothers*, the *expectation* of domestic integrity is confounded by the *reality* of the gang members' deaths. The audience is disturbed because—"them folks what was killed," i.e., a "family," somehow alienated from the grandiose crimes they commit. The sense of foul play over the not very remarkable execution of two murders is, at basis, an expression of indignation at the punishment of the "family," which has, after all, upheld domestic values even if they did break society's larger taboos.

In this context, the opposition between the gang and the "law" can be thought of as the opposition between the clan and society: the primitive, rurally-based tribe and the urban-centered society which evolved out of it. And if sentiments are thrown to the clan in *Bonnie and Clyde*, for reasons which will be discussed later, in the traditional Western, society must kill the clan lest, as every schoolboy knows, the gang destroy the town (or society). Moreover, the bank which every gang aspires to rob is a symbol that gives the "game" away: implicit in the pooled wealth is the individual's agreement to give up his tribal allegiance by storing his valuables with society rather than with the "father" of the clan.

For the Barrow gang, robbing banks is "fun" precisely because they are a clan; they cannot feel guilty about breaking laws which, anthropologically speaking, postdate them. Instead, they are governed by their own domestic "rules" or better yet, by a modification of the primitive taboos of the archetypal clan described by Freud in *Totem and Taboo:* the prohibitions against incest and patricide. In films about Western outlaws, we notice a solidarity the "law" cannot touch until the primitive taboos are violated. Thus, the incest taboo is broken when the leader's moll is unfaithful, often with a lesser member of the gang. Patricide is attempted when a member tries to kill the leader in a bid for power, or to get the moll, or to receive a larger share of the spoils. Often the violation of these prohibitions leads directly to a change in allegiance from the clan to society when the "squealer" informs the "law" of the leader's whereabouts.

These gangland taboos are modified in *Bonnie and Clyde* by the domestic comedy "rules" imposed upon them. The prohibition against incest becomes a prohibition against sexuality—the hero's impotence force him and his girl to live together like brother and sister. "I'm your family," Clyde tells Bonnie, who adds "I've no Mamma now." The Barrow brothers become a self-sufficient unit who take on the roles—not of lovers—but of the kin their women were forced to leave. Significantly, Blanche calls Buck "Daddy," transferring to her husband the tie she once had with her minister-father. Similarly, patricide is so inconceivable within the domestic setting that it must be turned into its opposite. Unlike the Western gang, whose members are often kept from violence only by the leader's forcefulness, Clyde, Buck, and Clyde's alter ego—C. W. Moss—throw *mock* punches, play checkers, and take each other's photographs. The prohibition against killing the father-leader evolves as filial affection in which brotherly love overcompensates for any remnants of the original hatred. Love and the absence of sexual provocation: these are the elements which keep the family intact in *Blondie* as well as in *Bonnie and Clyde.*

The car, in this context, is used not only to parody the horse and stagecoach of the Western, but also as the *container* which alienates the clan from society. In fact, it is only when the members of the gang leave the car, or open its door in Bonnie's case, that they are killed. Fundamentally, the car divides society into units of five or six people, and when it is in motion, there is no *verbal* means of communicating with the inhabitants—the cars of the Barrow gang have no radios, for instance. Thus they are far more effectively self-contained than in their motel rooms, where grocery boys can knock on the door. Because society's aim is to breach the small unit, the "law" tends to shoot at the car, at times, in preference to the gang itself, and thus, appropriately, one of the last shots in the film is a study of the bullet holes in the "dead" car.

In the end, Bonnie and Clyde die, not because they rob and murder but because they break the archetypal clan taboos and themselves dissolve their domestic solidarity. The agent of their "sin" is, specifically, the newspaper—society's representative. The Barrow gang's fatal mistake is to allow the newspaper into the car, a leverage for society which eventually destroys them. At first, the newspapers are treated as a joke—the Barrow gang laugh when accused of crimes they could not possibly commit. But the joke has soured by the time of Buck's death when an article hints that Clyde left his brother to die. Because the suggestion of fratricide (a nominal form of patricide) has an element of truth in it, Clyde gets angry at the newspaper, an indication that society has at last made its will felt. The taboo against sexuality, furthermore, is broken after Bonnie's poem is published in the newspaper. "You've made something out of me," Clyde says immediately before his first sexual contact with Bonnie. The *fact* of the poem's publication implies that the gang leader has accepted the social recognition which is inimical to domestic prohibitions. The final dissolution of the gang occurs, of course, when the "squealers"—C. W.'s father and Blanche— make personal contact with the "law," changing their allegiance from clan to society. In the attempt of C. W.'s father to get a mild sentence for his son and in Blanche's attempt to justify Buck, the clan's taboos are replaced by society's.

The meaning of Bonnie and Clyde's death is, then, a reaffirmation of society's right to preserve its own structure, *even* at the expense of the primitive (and "innocent") family integrity. The choice is given between the civilized, if brutal, town and the childlike, rustic "paradise," with the advantage always given to the former. In the film, the break-up of the clan is represented by the image of glass shattered. The opening shot of Bonnie's lips seen in a mirror is contrasted by the last shot of the car windows smashed by bullets. Significantly, glass is most often shattered by violence when the "law" confronts the gang—windows are broken, mirrors, windshields, and so forth. But the symbol is used both ways: the farmer whose property is confiscated by the bank (society) shoots the windows of his farmhouse in a largely ineffectual gesture of retribution. Here the puniness of the small man's (and the clan's) destructive intent is heightened in a contrast with the long panning shot of the town's intact glass storefronts, ending at the window of "Eva's Ice Cream Parlor"—the rendezvous of the "squealer" and the "law."

Arthur Penn's obsessive shots of glass are also evident in his playful use of sunglasses. The Greek punishment for the breaker of taboos, blindness, is used in the film in the literal blinding of Blanche (who wears dark glasses) and in the figurative blinding of Clyde, who is wearing *shattered* sunglasses when he dies. In fact, eyes, which are more or less the "windows" separating one human being from another, are especially important in the role of Clyde. Warren Beatty tells a truth with his eyes that is often antithetical to the less honest animation of his hands or to his words. Moreover, Clyde's "sense" of the "law," which often saves the gang, is really his ability to *sight* danger, an ability he forfeits when he wears the broken sunglasses. Blindness becomes the ultimate shattering of the fragile barrier between clan and society, a shattering which virtually means the death of the clan, and which began when their first victim was fatally blinded after being shot through a car window.

Like glass, the camera lens serves as a link between the clan and society. In photographs the Barrow gang assume the pretense of the threat society considers them, rather than the domestic innocents they represent within their own setting. For all the gang's mimicry in front of the camera, the lens records a truth beyond the local occasion: the danger of the small unit when its power is not absorbed by the large.

This danger was particularly felt in the 1930's, when banks failed and society threatened to disintegrate. The film's fascination with the fourth decade of this century is not merely a recreation of a "camp" era; it is fully justified in terms of the film's theme. Because of poverty, the natural barrier between society and the clan threatened to shatter in the Thirties. As the film emphasizes, people were forming tribal allegiances when the "law" failed them. The sequences involving Bonnie's family reunion and the squatters who give the gang water are shot as exteriors with no man-made structure in view—a return to the prenativity of civilization which is quite at odds with the highly developed towns and their huge glass storefronts. The new emergence of the small unit during the Depression has previously been best represented in films by the small man in the role of gangster—Paul Muni, James Cagney, Edward G.

Robinson—but Arthur Penn's great achievement in *Bonnie and Clyde* is the use of the domestic comedy—Western as another way of expressing the tension between tribe and town. From this anthropological point of view, the film works beautifully, although its final critical success depends on the extent to which the psychological motivation of the characters coincides with the larger theme. The return of Clyde's potency, for instance, may be explained as the breaking of an archetypal taboo, but it is not quite believable in terms of the character Warren Beatty creates.

Nevertheless, the film's immediate impact suggests its relevance to the present: the 1960's will no doubt be remembered as the decade when urbanization back-fired: when society again threatened to break up into small units that periodically riot and loot and have "fun" doing so. The Barrow gang's closest counterpart today may perhaps be found in Negro ghettos, where local taboos have replaced social law and order.

Aesthetic and Moral Value in
BONNIE AND CLYDE
by WILLIAM J. FREE

Bonnie and Clyde has become the *cause célèbre* of contemporary American film making. It provokes reactions—violent, often startling, usually paradoxical. Professional critics and public alike are sharply divided concerning its merits. Is it a cheap and tawdry glorification of crime and immorality, or is it one of the landmarks in the art of the American cinema? The argument rages in terms that extreme.

The most important thing, perhaps, is that here is an American film which deserves the close analysis usually reserved for literary works, more serious drama, and the films of European directors like Bergman, Fellini, and Antonioni. *Bonnie and Clyde* is undoubtedly a work of art of quality and wide appeal (witness its effect on fashion, television commercials, and other motion pictures). Yet the criticism of the film (negative and positive) has occurred on strangely irrelevant grounds. Bosley Crowther of the *New York Times* panned the film because it is not an accurate portrayal of the real Bonnie Parker and Clyde Barrow and presented extensive documentation to support his case.[1] Unfortunately, most of the letters answering Crowther defend the film for the equally pointless reason that it accurately pictures life during the depression. Neither side seemed willing to deal with the film as a work of art, a failing which perhaps

From the Quarterly Journal of Speech *54 (October 1968): 220–25. Reprinted by permission of the* Quarterly Journal of Speech *and the author.*

[1] *New York Times*, September 3, 1967, II and X, pp. 1 and 10. For numerous letters reacting to Crowther's review see the *New York Times*, September 17, 1967, II, pp. 7 and 9.

stems naturally from its use of historical characters as sources. But even critics who do deal with the film on its own terms, such as Richard Gilman of the *New Republic*, find it a contradiction of moods and ultimately flawed.[2]

One cause of the difficulty, I believe, comes from the fact that in its structure *Bonnie and Clyde* is radically unlike our expectations. It is built on a peculiar relationship of aesthetic and moral values which gives it its tremendous emotional impact and makes it a film of significance. In this essay I would like to examine that structure and its importance.

Bonnie and Clyde works within the conventions of the most violent subgenre of the film: the American gangster movie of the 1930's. Gun battles from speeding automobiles, police sieges of motel cabins, rattling tommy guns, these stocks-in-trade of the gangster film to which most of us ceased to react at about the age of fifteen are also the stock-in-trade of *Bonnie and Clyde*. Yet here they evoke a fresh emotional reaction which our recognition of their stereotyped nature partially supports. The reaction is artfully achieved. The nature of its artistry is to gain our sympathies for the characters by using aesthetic values to obscure moral values, then to reassert the latent moral values with an enormous impact which is strengthened by the fact that they have lain dormant throughout most of the film.

In order to see *Bonnie and Clyde* clearly, we must keep moral and aesthetic values in art distinct and examine their interaction. By moral values I mean character in the Aristotelian sense: that is, the "moral purpose" revealed by "what kind of things a man chooses or avoids." [3] By aesthetic values I mean those elements of form and style in which the work is created: the style of language (or in the case of film, pictures) in which the work is told, the techniques for achieving unity and emphasis, the sequence in which events are presented—all the purely "formal" aspects of the work.

In the first half of the film Bonnie and Clyde live in a comic world, a world of pure style, of pure aesthetic value. It is comic in two ways. First, their picaresque, nomadic life develops an Arcadian pastoral quality. Walter Kerr has recently said that the automobile perfectly symbolizes the film because it frees the driver from the

[2] "Gangsters on the Road to Nowhere," *New Republic* (November 4, 1967), pp. 27–29.

[3] Aristotle's *Poetics*, VI, 17. Butcher translation.

confines of time, space, and society just as the montage of individual frames of film is free from similar restrictions.[4] Bonnie and Clyde live in their automobiles, running from a society in which they are misfits. They create their own mobile world with its own values. If we accept these values as they are presented, we achieve an identity with their freedom from and hostility toward the mechanical and solemn world against which they rebel.[5] They become folk heroes, an identity which the film suggests by the reaction of the poor and downtrodden toward them, by their own acts of Robin Hood justice as they let individuals keep their own money and steal only from banks, and by the spirited banjo music which accompanies their travels. Like Jim and Huck moving between the freedom of the raft and the corruption of the shore, Bonnie and Clyde move from automobile to bank.

The society against which they rebel is so sketchily represented that it can in no way gain our sympathy. In the first half of the film Bonnie and Clyde encounter not people but institutions drawn in the broadest and most comic way. We totally sympathize with the freedom and exuberance of their automobile world. We identify with the *style* of their life. This identity obscures the moral implications of the fact that they are committing crimes. Because they are alive and the other world is essentially dead, we accept their values.

Second, they are comic in their inability to achieve success in their chosen world. Clyde is farcically unable to succeed as a criminal in spite of his obvious criminal inclinations. They are inept players of a game of cops and robbers which is more like a Keystone Cops farce than like reality. In one sequence Clyde robs a bank which had recently failed. He forces the single remaining teller to go to the car and explain to Bonnie so that she will not accuse him of getting cold feet. In this sequence, we see Clyde become the comic fool— the man who in his attempt to profane the existing order is exposed as a bubbling and impotent imposter. Similar examples of the criminal as fool abound throughout the first half of the film. Clyde

---

[4] "The Movies Are Better Than the Theater," *New York Times Magazine,* March 3, 1968, p. 41.

[5] In an interview published since this article was written, director Arthur Penn confirms my reading of the comic intention of this part of the film. He says: "We used laughter to get the audience to feel like a member of the gang, to have the feeling of adventure, a feeling of playing together." See "Bonnie and Clyde," *Evergreen Review,* No. 55 (June 1968), p. 62. [See this volume, pp. 15–19.]

is attacked by a grocer with a meat cleaver in an unsuccessful robbery attempt; C. W. Moss wedges the getaway car into a tight parallel parking place during an attempted bank robbery; Clyde's voice fails when he announces a stickup to a bankful of people, and he must repeat himself to get attention; and, at the beginning, Clyde meets Bonnie as she foils his attempt to steal her mother's car.

During the first half of the film we see no instance of a successful crime. Clyde's image as fool is strengthened by his incredulous reactions to his own failure. After being attacked by the grocer, he exclaims: "Try to get something to eat in this town and some son of a bitch attacks you with a meat cleaver." The irony of his moral indignation further identifies him as the fool who is not only a bungler but blind to the reality of his own identity. In each of these instances, the failure of the characters to achieve their goals as criminals provides a tone of comic absurdity which, along with our sympathy for the style of their Arcadian life, endears them to us.

Thus the first half of the film creates a comic world so entertaining and engaging to us that its aesthetic values neutralize if not reverse our normal moral judgments of the actions of its characters. This reversal of moral norms provides the film with what Bertolt Brecht called the "alienation-effect" (*Verfremdungseffekt*). According to Brecht, "a representation that alienates is one which allows us to recognize its subject, but at the same time makes it seem unfamiliar." [6] *Bonnie and Clyde* uses its *Verfremdungseffekt* to lift our reaction to violence from the stereotyped to the cathartic. We recognize the subject—a gangster film—but the values presented on the screen are so different from our stereotyped expectations that we see the subjects in a new light.

The last hour of the film systematically undercuts the comic world and asserts an underlying moral necessity, culminating in the horrifying blood bath at the end. The seeds of its destruction inhere in the comic world itself. Paradoxically, as they succeed in the world and are transformed from its fools into its heroes, Bonnie and Clyde become subject to its morality. Only so long as they are the bungling fools in a comic world of their own are they free to live their Arcadian mobile existence. Success destroys Arcadia and substitutes reality.

The turning point of the film is the bank robbery sequence in

---

[6] *Brecht on Theatre*, ed. John Willett (New York, 1964), p. 192.

which C. W. Moss wedges the car into the parking place. The scene is the high point of the comic world—the Barrow gang looking vainly up and down the street for their getaway car, Moss frantically smashing into the cars in front of and behind him trying to free himself from his predicament, the two Negroes leaning on the wall watching impassively. Then, as the gang makes its successful getaway, a bank guard jumps onto the back of the car and Clyde shoots him in the face. The sudden and gruesome flash of blood marks their success, their elevation from fools to heroes in their chosen world, and the beginning of their downfall. It adumbrates Buck's horrible death from a similar wound at the movie's end.

Their Arcadian world is ruined. The next sequence shows Clyde reprimanding the distraught Moss in a movie theatre while Bonnie tries to escape from their success in the gaudy world of a 1930's musical, with a succession of overdressed chorus girls parading across the screen singing, ironically, "We're in the Money." Reality has broken into their gay, childish rapport. Although the comic mood reaches beyond this point, it never again dominates the tone of the film.

More and more incidents undercut the comic style as the film progresses. Particularly, Bonnie serves as a figure of dissatisfaction with the quality of their lives. She grows restless at the life of hamburgers and french fries on the run, dirty motel rooms with five occupants and no privacy, the self-righteous nagging of Buck's preacher's-daughter wife, and, most of all, the alienation from her family, particularly from her mother. The attempt to maintain the Arcadian world becomes strident. Reminders of reality begin to creep in. The happy trick of photographing the Texas Ranger with the Barrow gang collapses when he spits in Bonnie's face and the prank explodes into Clyde's almost insane violence. Their gay sociability with the kidnapped couple (their only contact with people outside their own world) withers when Bonnie learns that he is an undertaker and thus a reminder of the fatal necessity underlying their existence. Bonnie has joined Clyde to escape. As the film progresses, she finds herself more and more trapped. The comic world slowly decays.

Bonnie's ultimate recognition of the finality of her choice comes in the scene in which she visits her mother. The family picnic on the barren sand hill with C. W. Moss standing guard over the group with a shotgun, its pathetic attempt to achieve gaiety amid gaunt emptiness, is Bonnie's last feeble attempt to avoid the reality of her world. When she expresses her desire to live near her mother, the woman answers, "You'll be dead if you do." Moments later Clyde states that they do the best they can. Robbery is how they make money. There is no exit from their chosen world. In the next sequence the siege of the motel bursts onto the screen and violence thereafter dominates the film.

The three sequences in which the gang is destroyed are perhaps the most brutally violent ever filmed. Buck, blood flowing from the temple wound; his wife, blinded by a shotgun blast and screaming hysterically because she knows her husband is dying; these scenes transform the automobile from Arcadia into Hell. The ambush in the clearing animates the automobile into a trapped animal as Clyde tries to drive through the ring of gunfire only to find himself blocked at every turn. And everywhere blood. Blood streaming down Clyde's wounded arm. Blood spreading across the back of Bonnie's water-soaked dress. Blood covering Buck and his wife as he dies surrounded by the police. And finally the slow-motion of the last scene, Clyde rolled in the dust like the tin can which the western hero uses to demonstrate his marksmanship; Bonnie in her slow dance of death, jerking as the bullets strike her body.

But these graphic details of violence, however great, do not suffice to account for the powerful emotional effect of the movie. The horror of that effect is stronger than simple nausea at the profusion of blood. It can be explained, I think, only through the relationship between the comic Arcadian world of the first half of the film and the moral intent that runs throughout it and emerges in full force only at the end.

The conclusion of *Bonnie and Clyde* approaches the catharsis of tragedy. Its structure bears a close analogy to that of tragedy.

The tragic hero is a man who suffers violence because he succeeds in achieving his chosen identity, an identity which we can admire and with which we can empathize, yet an identity which presupposes the eventuality of violence. Hamlet achieves identity as an avenger and dies; Macbeth becomes king and dies; Oedipus learns who he is and suffers; Agamemnon becomes the conquerer and dies. Each of them seeks a being which the audience approves; yet suffering and death are necessary ingredients of this being itself. In their suffering we recognize the unbending fate underlying mankind. That recognition produces the catharsis of which Aristotle speaks.

The comic world of the first half of *Bonnie and Clyde* is so attractive and happy that we aspire to its gaiety and identify with its style. Certainly we admire Bonnie and Clyde for their aspirations to that world, particularly when we see it juxtaposed to the real world. The old, slovenly, ugly waitress who serves them in the hamburger joint early in the film; the haggard, defeated farm families with whom they constantly come in contact; these describe the real world which lay in store for Bonnie and Clyde. The real world is death; the Arcadian criminal world is life. *As it is presented to us,* we must admire their choice of the latter and aspire to it with them.

Thus the "tragedy" follows inevitably from their choice of life. Having chosen this identity, they are as doomed as Hamlet after he surrenders to his identity as avenger. Success as a criminal means violent death.

But here is the twist upon which the whole film turns. We don't know that until it is too late. And neither does Bonnie. We and Bonnie are seduced into an unreal world. We enjoy the ride. After Clyde "robs" the failed bank, we and Bonnie laugh together at his rage as he fires an impotent bullet through the plate glass window and we are still laughing as he drives away. Success isn't necessary for Bonnie and us; love takes its place, her love for Clyde, ours for the madcap world into which we have been drawn. So we both blind ourselves to the implications of the identity which we have chosen.

But Clyde knows. The genius of Warren Beatty's portrayal is his ability to communicate to us the seething need for violence under his surface. Clyde must be successfully violent to have an identity. He has cut off two toes to escape a work detail and get parole, but more important, I think, because it is only in such a violent act that he can express his being. The theme of his sexual impotence carries much of the burden of this being. So long as he is a failure, he is impotent. He becomes sexually alive only after first he has tasted violence himself—has been wounded seriously trying to escape—and second after his success is assured by Bonnie's poem in the newspaper. And the last line of the poem is "And they died." Clyde is now real. He is alive. And he never apologizes for his choice. When Bonnie at one point asks him what he would do differently if he had it all to do over he says, "I wouldn't live in the same state where we pull our jobs."

The impact of the final violence comes from the fact that we come for the first time face to face with reality. Like Bonnie escaping into the world of the musical movie, we have escaped into Bonnie and Clyde's movie world. Its comedy has made us forget the reality of violence. We have been taken in. And then the movie slaps us across the face and says, "Look, this is how it really is." Comedy has so blunted our stereotyped responses that it is like looking at violence for the first time.

This is why I would contend that the movie is essentially moral. At the end our moral values are restored with a shock. No sane person, I contend, could experience the film and aspire to the life it describes. The ultimate effect is not to make crime attractive but to make violence horrible. More than this, it achieves a near-tragic catharsis. We see people we admire suffer and die because of what they are.

In order to achieve catharsis, we must identify with the characters. What makes *Bonnie and Clyde* interesting and significant is that it achieves our empathy by aesthetic rather than moral means. All tragic heroes commit evil deeds: Oedipus kills his father and marries his mother, Hamlet and Macbeth murder kings, Orestes kills his mother. But each of these has redeeming moral qualities which elevate him in our estimation. Even in the conventional American gangster film the antihero possesses moral strengths which involve us with him in spite of his evil deeds. The popularity of Humphrey Bogart illustrates the fact. The 1930's vintage gangster film which perhaps came closest to tragedy was Bogart's *High Sierra*. Bogart's portrayal achieved our empathy because of the man's strength, courage, and sensitivity, particularly at the end of the film as he realizes that he is doomed by his chosen way of life. But there, too, our empathy is gained by moral means, a mixture of good and evil which is indigenous to all tragedy.

Bonnie and Clyde gains our empathy through purely aesthetic means. The comic vitality of their way of life, not any attractive moral qualities of their characters, attracts us to them. They are "beautiful people" leading beautiful lives for a long and happy hour. Unlike most tragic characters, their moral qualities are not destroyed by their evil; their beautiful world is destroyed by ugliness, the ugliness of violence. Morality is not a raw material in *Bonnie and Clyde;* beauty and ugliness are. But the shock of pity and fear on confronting the ultimate reality of death is a moral effect. We shrink in horror from violent death and from the fate which has led Bonnie and Clyde to it. Such a reaction is moral in the highest sense.

Whether or not *Bonnie and Clyde* is a true tragedy can be disputed. Some may argue that there is no recognition on the part of the characters. The recognition is shifted to the spectator in the poignant scene in town just before the conclusion. For a brief moment, Bonnie and Clyde are like any other loving young couple in town on Saturday afternoon to do the shopping. We recognize them as like ourselves. Yet we know they are about to be ambushed. At this moment, I think, we recognize the moral falsity of the world into which we have been drawn. Here is another reality, a reality of domestic tranquility, of quiet everyday moments. But it is not reality for Bonnie and Clyde. They have chosen the exciting life which we have shared with them, and now they are about to reap its rewards. Here is the moment of moral recognition for the audience. We see that these beautiful people and their beautiful world are essentially false. Like them, we have been drawn into beauty; like them, we must suffer the ugliness which is its brother. Wisely, the film ends with gunfire and with the lawmen standing solemnly over the bodies.

Our Film and Theirs:
GRAPES OF WRATH
and
BONNIE AND CLYDE
by JOHN HOWARD LAWSON

I have been asked to write on *What is happening in film.* A great deal is happening, in the United States and throughout the world. In Hollywood, there are more than forty percent unemployed, while young Americans try to use film to portray their contemporary experience, their rage against injustice, their hatred of war.

I have decided to avoid the difficulties of generalizing about a few or a score of films. I believe it will be more fruitful to consider two motion pictures, *The Grapes of Wrath* in 1940 and *Bonnie and Clyde* in 1967. In doing so, I shall raise some questions about the responsibility of film to history, the changes in cinematic thought and in general culture during these crucial years.

Radicals of my generation who cherish the memory of the thirties may feel that it is blasphemous to compare the two pictures. They will exclaim, in Hamlet's words to his mother:

Look here upon this picture and on this—
. . . Have you eyes

But what we *see* on the screen does not depend solely on the testimony of our eyes. The *inner eye* responds to the pattern of sight

From American Dialogue *5 (Winter 1968–69): 30–33. Reprinted by permission of* American Dialogue.

and sound in terms of each person's sensibility and modes of thought. *Bonnie and Clyde* appeals to young people and is credited with having brought a large number of them back to the theatres. It strikes a responsive chord, communicating something about the thirties and about today which is meaningful to many spectators. We cannot ignore this meaning, nor can we doubt the serious intentions of the artists who made the film. Its director, Arthur Penn, is exceptionally gifted and has done distinguished work in theatre and film. *Bonnie and Clyde* has won ten nominations for Academy awards.

The Grapes of Wrath begins in the same territory—the roads and farms of Oklahoma, Texas and neighboring states. The depression background is similar, although *Bonnie and Clyde* takes place at an earlier date, ending with the killing of the two outlaws in May, 1934. Steinbeck's book, published in 1939, reflects the emphasis on social organization and the hope of progress which were to some extent characteristic of the late thirties. However, it would be a mistake to view *The Grapes of Wrath* as typical of the film culture of its time. It was an exception to the commercial run-of-the-mill production of violent westerns, gangster stories, tawdry musicals. *Gone with the Wind,* with its vulgar racism, had its première in Atlanta, Georgia, a few months before the release of *Grapes of Wrath.* The film industry's insensitivity to Negro protest is demonstrated by the well-publicized revival of *Gone with the Wind* in the spring of 1968.

Gone with the Wind may help to remind us that there are many links between the dominant culture of the thirties and the trends of American thought thirty years later.

The film adaptation of *Grapes of Wrath,* written by Nunally Johnson and directed by John Ford, has a simpler structure than the novel and is less concerned with fundamental social change. The resemblances to *Bonnie and Clyde* are striking not only in locale but in the portrayal of dispossessed farmers, the documentary approach, the form of the narrative as a journey, the emphasis on family ties, the social commentary on poor people driven to desperation in a sick society.

The film, *Grapes of Wrath,* reaches a climax when Tom Joad becomes a murderer and outlaw. Seeing his friend, Casey, murdered by a deputy, Tom kills the officer with a pickhandle. Tom says goodby to his mother: "Sooner or later, they'll get me. But long as I'm an outlaw, anyway, maybe I can do sump'n . . . I'll be all around in the dark. . . . Wherever there's a fight so hungry people can eat, I'll be there." The mother says, "I don't understand it," and Tom answers, "Me neither." Bonnie's mother says the same words to her daughter in their last moment together.

There is an obvious difference between Tom Joad's belief in brotherhood and Clyde Barrow's murderous career. If Tom's spirit is still around, it is with the agricultural workers in Delano, California. Yet, in spite of this connection between the social struggles of the thirties and the sixties, it must be admitted that *The Grapes of Wrath* has a viewpoint and style which seem remote, and—what is worse!—irrelevant to many Americans, including young dissenters who find our society intolerable. To these same people, *Bonnie and Clyde* has something urgent to say. An English critic calls it "a film for now, and perhaps for posterity." [1]

The makers of the picture were consciously concerned with its social meaning. Warren Beatty, who produced it and plays the role of Clyde, says of the lovers: "The particular relationship between them interests me less than the relationship of the two of them to their society and the times." Arthur Penn says he is "worried about what is happening in the country. . . . I remember a very militant and vivid time during the depression when I was growing up." Bonnie and Clyde, according to the director, should be seen as "historical figures in the social-political situation in which they found themselves. . . . It was a paralyzed country." [2]

In view of these declarations, the film demands analysis of its use of research and its treatment of the characters as "historical figures." It was made in the area where Bonnie and Clyde lived, and many people who had known them were interviewed. David Benton, who wrote the script with Bob Newman, grew up in a small Texas town and had heard innumerable stories about the fugitives.

Most of the situations in the film are reproduced in detail from the story told by Bonnie's mother and Clyde's sister in a book published in 1934.[3] But there is one decisive deviation from the relatives' account: the opening of the picture and the meeting of the lovers do not conform to the facts. Bonnie met Clyde when she was visiting a friend in West Dallas in January 1930. Although she was only

---

[1] Gordon Gow, in *Films and Filming*, London, October, 1967.
[2] Interviews with Warren Beatty and Arthur Penn, by Curtis Lee Hansen, in *Cinema*, Beverly Hills, Summer, 1967.
[3] *Ibid.*, pp. 61–62.

twenty, she had been married four years to a man named Roy
Thornton. They had broken up, and he had been sentenced to
prison.

Clyde had minor trouble with the law, but Bonnie believed he
would go straight and urged him to do so. When he was arrested in
February 1930, she wrote him: "Sugar, when you get out, I want you
to go to work. . . . I am almost worried to death about this." [4]
When he was sent to the state prison at Huntsville, Texas, she wrote
him passionate, childish letters, and his replies address her as "My
darling little wife," although they were not legally married. When
he was released in February, 1932, his sister found him completely
changed. He tried to tell her why, relating incidents in the penitentiary: he had been close by when an older prisoner knifed a
young boy to death, and the murderer received only minor punishment. There is no mention of homosexuality, but what we know of
prison life suggests a homosexual situation.

The film opens in a way which eliminates this background. With
the credit titles, there are photographs of the period, establishing a
tone which is both comic and documentary. There is a startling
transition to a closeup of Bonnie's lips. She is naked in bed; from
her window she sees a stranger about to steal a car. She calls to
him, and puts on her dress as she hurries down the stairs. Clyde tells
her he has served two years for armed robbery. He shows her his
gun, an obvious sex symbol. In order to impress her, he holds up a
store. Then a car careens down a road. Clyde is trying to drive while
Bonnie is embracing him in a frenzy of sexual excitement.

The effect of this opening is to cancel all the motivations that
actually existed for the conduct of Bonnie and Clyde. There is no
time for them to fall in love. They move by blind impulse: all that
Bonnie cares about is that the man has and uses a gun: sex and
aggression are identical, and the concurrence of the two drives unites
them immediately and forever.

This is all very modern. It is not my purpose here to debate the
psychological interaction of sexual pathology and aggressive or criminal conduct. The connection is well known, and has been studied
by social scientists and reported in newspaper headlines. I am concerned with its use here as a catchall premise that undermines the

---

[4] *The Story of Clyde Barrow and Bonnie Parker*, as told by Mrs. Emma Parker
and Nell Barrow Cowan, compiled and edited by Jan I. Fortune, Dallas, 1934.
[See this volume, pp. 122–23.]

sense of the story and destroys its structure. The haste and hysteria of the opening exclude other considerations, and lead to nothing but flight and gun-battles. Their doom is sealed before we have met them—or before they really met each other.

The film has what might be called a circular form—the end is contained in the beginning. There can be no development: the cinematic impact lies in the juxtaposition of scenes of love or family affection with bloody gun-battles. This is the meaning of the film: people are both normal and absurdly violent. The Barrow gang are no worse—and probably a great deal better—than the law officers who pursue them. The film could not convey its meaning if it tried to transcend these limits—because these limits *are* its meaning.

It is the first American film which expresses total alienation. It differs from European portrayals of a lifeless society (Truffaut's *Fahrenheit 451*, Godard's *Alphaville*) in that the characters are very much alive in their sealed and desperate condition. There is a limited truth in this. Bonnie and Clyde try to make some kind of sense out of a crazy society, but they are so much a part of it that they are trapped absurdly, monstrously.

There is no doubt that the film is an attack on American society, linking the evils of the thirties with the continuing predominance of oppression, corruption and hypocrisy in the present. But the elements of truth in the story are all on the surface. It cannot probe beneath the surface without contradicting its premise—that everybody is both psychopathic and decent, because the social order is an asylum in which the keepers are crazier than the patients.

There is no psychological depth in the portraits of Bonnie and Clyde. This is crudely indicated in the fact that Clyde is impotent. At the beginning he tells her, "I'm not much of a lover boy." But how does it affect a girl who is wildly in love? Apparently it has no serious effect. It is simply a condition, an aspect of alienation. Toward the end, Clyde overcomes his deficiency—apparently this is a final irony: they are able to be normal when it is too late.

Faye Dunaway, analyzing her role, says that "Bonnie is really a schizophrenic personality—a girl who uses a machine gun and tries to write poetry." [5] But which side of her is morally commendable —the machine gun or the poetry? Underlying the question is one of the fundamental questions of our time: what is the distinction be-

[5] *Los Angeles Times,* West magazine, March 10, 1968.

tween socially motivated violence and criminal violence? The film assumes that there is no distinction. It goes even further and tells us that the lovers are morally justified. Arthur Penn speaks of "the bravura with which they decided to assault the system." Penn admits that the real Bonnie and Clyde lacked heroic stature. But he says: "I wish that Bonnie and Clyde had it, and I certainly mean that they should have it in the film." [6]

This conception carries us to the ultimate limits of alienation. In an age when anti-heroes proliferate, a return to heroism is welcome. But the truth is that heroism is an ethical concept. There is no morality in *Bonnie and Clyde,* and therefore there is no compassion. It is romantic to talk about their bravura: We can have compassion for them if we look upon them as pitiful victims. They are not rebels, for they accept all the false values of their society. Even their love for their mothers, which is touching, expresses their dependence, their inability to become adults. The book which purports to tell their true story asserts that the time they spent as fugitives "were the most horrible years ever spent by young people." [7] The film cannot recognize this horror. Yet it is important for Americans today to realize that this horror existed in the thirties, that it was a time when Robinson Jeffers could write:

> Blind war, compared to this kind of life,
> Has nobility, famine has dignity.[8]

I doubt whether many of us today can believe that war and famine are better than the deadening routine of American life. But we know, more clearly than we knew in the thirties, that the power structure in our country feeds on war and exploits hunger.

The homeless farmers who appear in *Bonnie and Clyde* are more like the Joads than like the outlaws. They were more rebellious than the youngsters making unsuccessful raids on banks. But the later film performs a service in reminding us that the moral crisis in the United States today has a history, and is related to the guns-and-money culture of the thirties. One of the most significant scenes in *Bonnie and Clyde,* following a hold-up of a bank and its "absurd" and bloody aftermath, shows them hiding in a film theatre. Clyde is

[6] Interview in *Cinema,* quoted above.
[7] p. III.
[8] Robinson Jeffers, *Solstice and Other Poems,* 1935.

arguing with one of his followers, but Bonnie is engrossed in *Gold Diggers of 1933,* an elaborate production number, "We're in the money," shows the screen filled with monstrous coins.

Penn speaks of the story of the lovers as a legend, especially in the small towns around Dallas. I wonder whether they are remembered because they were "rebels" or because they committed fourteen murders. In the film, we see them die under a rain of machine-gun bullets. But two hours afterward there is a scene which does not appear in the picture: a crowd had gathered, and "Bonnie's dress, which was shot to ribbons, was almost cut from her back by curiosity seekers. Clyde's bloodstained shirt and undershirt were in the same condition. Bonnie's hair had been clipped away also, and someone was trying to get her diamond rings off her fingers." [9]

Perhaps the film would have been closer to the truth if it had included this scene.

[9] From the book by her mother and his sister, p. 250.

The Good-Bad and Bad-Good in Movies:
BONNIE AND CLYDE
and IN COLD BLOOD
by ROBERT STEELE

This article has as its impetus a conversation between Richard Schickel, film critic for *Life,* and Bosley Crowther, former film critic for *The New York Times.* Our meeting took place after their sparring in print about their different evaluations of *Bonnie and Clyde.* Schickel maintained that a film-maker has a right and a responsibility to reflect his times and that because our times are violent, there is no choice but to present violence in films. Crowther did not disagree about the prevalence of violence but felt that *Bonnie and Clyde* had gone beyond the bounds of good taste and judgment in the way it presented these killers. I made the following transcript of Crowther's longest contribution to the conversation:

I don't want to sound like a Puritan, but I think it is our responsibility as critics to call the turn on so many pictures that appear to be in a popular mood of liberated young people. They feel that the establishment has failed us and that they must be permitted to have their own values.

Leadership and responsibility cannot be expected of very young critics. They are unaware of the wars we have gone through

From The Catholic World, *May 1968, pp. 76–80. Reprinted by permission of* The Catholic World *and the author.*

in order to liberate the screen, and . . . for the liberation of honest values. *Sound of Music* is like *Bonnie and Clyde* in being close to a kind of immorality. *Sound of Music* gives a romanticized, sugary, unreal notion of ideal behavior.

Schickel agreed with Crowther in damning *Sound of Music*. Crowther went on to say that *"Bonnie and Clyde* gives a false impression of the basic nature and attitudes of people who fall into criminal life—making it a playful, fun way of life. It is immoral, and we have to say so. Getting moral content into pictures is not the responsibility of the code or of censorship, but it is the responsibility of those who make pictures. And it is our responsibility to tell them when we think they are going wrong. The film critic is performing a function akin to a pastor. He is a counsellor of a community about the values of a picture. . . ."

Crowther said that what he is most against is "violence dragged in for its own sake. We have experienced the violence of last summer. We live in these times, and it is the duty of the film-maker to examine our times. Our work should be to give a blanket condemnation of sex and violence . . . rather we've opened up the screen so that we may deal with violence. The immorality I see is the cynical exploitation of violence."

Schickel, by being less vocal, may have been acknowledging his respect for the dean of American film critics' unquestioned sincerity and earnestness, but he would not concede to Crowther's main argument. He said, "The film critic has no business letting his morality shape his criticism. The critic should judge a film *vis à vis* other films of a comparable genre and not according to his moral preferences or prejudices."

Because I had not seen *Bonnie and Clyde* at the time, I made no contribution to the talk; but now, after having seen it three times, I feel that my hunch about what was missing in their consideration was accurate. Schickel would have been right if he were only referring to documentary films. Their business is to reflect life. But the stance of Arthur Penn, the director of *Bonnie and Clyde*, was, rightly, not to reflect life; he used the raw material of history to create a film with artistic aims. Crowther was right to the extent that films are more vehicles of communication than objects of art which manufacture attitudes and values of individuals and, consequently, of society. But both Crowther and Schickel failed to give attention to whether the violence in the film deepens or limits its artistic merit.

As successful entertainment and something that gives the public what it wants to buy, *Bonnie and Clyde* is a triumph. Art *is* entertaining, and some entertainment may be art. The way an artist selects and handles his subject matter to create a certain kind of content is fundamental in getting at the artistic worth of a film. The artist gets a meaning out of his subject matter that enables his film to make a contribution to a larger and more durable world of values, insights, originality, and style than the routine movie which is as transient and disposable as a paper cup.

The fresh amalgam of the domestic-comedy, Western, and gangster movie routines make *Bonnie and Clyde* a dazzling picture, and something would be lacking in anyone who could keep from becoming deeply involved in it. This involvement explains the movie's tremendous popularity and success as well as the paucity of negative thought about what is going on beneath its surface. Anyone with reservations about the film is denounced as being morally offended. However, it is interesting to note that the Norwegians *have* been offended and have banned the film from their country because of its "brutality."

My own grievances against the film are more on artistic than on moral grounds. I don't think it will make bank robbers and killers of viewers who are not already somewhat disposed to or well along the path to violence. I realize that it does seem to be having this repercussion if one thinks of the new brash of robberies the newspapers associate with Bonnie and Clyde, the two criminals, and that *Bonnie and Clyde* type of larky fun and violence may increase if the film's multiple nominations for Academy Awards give it an Oscar landslide. Still, I think that it is primarily on artistic grounds that the film can be deemed pernicious.

Behind the opening credits of the film, we see bona fide snapshots of Bonnie and Clyde who are skillfully and sneakingly replaced in the photographs by Faye Dunaway and Warren Beatty. Unlike the two real-life characters, Dunaway and Beatty are attractive, likable, moral in a fictional way, and even good persons. Thus, we are not left to make up our minds about the real characters, as would be possible from a documented presentation of their escapades; we are railroaded into liking them, which we do. They don't really mean any harm. They are just like us: they want to get on—do something, amount to something—pit themselves against the doltishness of conventional law and order. They identify with all who are disposed to be individuals and outsiders—those who are an itch to the establishment. They mean well, but they don't think much; they just do "their thing." But sadly, their thing gets out of control. Then all they can do is what they are forced to do. All Clyde wants is a peach pie, and a "villain" comes up behind him with a butcher's cleaver. To save himself from this barbarian assault, he has to kill.

Even the less sensitive among us know when the film starts going sour and the trumping-up falters. Buck Barrow, Clyde's brother, a good fellow but not as attractive and appealing as Clyde, dies an agonizing and horrible death before our eyes, after he is hit by .38 caliber bullets. Blanche, his wife, is shot and says she's blinded. Bonnie and Clyde are both hit, covered with blood, look for all get out as if they are dying, but we find out later they just looked that way. They are ready to go again as soon as their arms are put into slings. C. W. drags them to safety, steals another car which, as usual, is standing nearby, all gassed up and battery o.k., and in a few seconds they all drive away. Even though we have just been through a sickening massacre, the same old jaunty banjo starts up again on the sound track. Previously, as an accompaniment to chases and getaways, it has charmed us into thinking that Bonnie and Clyde, wizards that they are, manage to turn their escapades into rollicking good times. But the use of this theme music to accompany a getaway with Bonnie and Clyde looking as if they were dead or dying in the back seat is an emotionally debauched moment in the film.

Because Bonnie and Clyde, by whom we are wooed and won, have to die, and death, *real* death, risks box-office death, we see them as dying and yet not really dying. The unreal ending of the film is anticipated by the sequence in which Bonnie meets her mother and relatives. And the washed-out color and slow motion of this sequence blatantly sets it outside of the rest of the film except for the ending. When Bonnie and Clyde finally die, their deaths are unlike all the previous deaths in the film, cinematically beautiful; they are shot in slow motion thus making them unreal when contrasted with the rest of the film. Thus the violence of their deaths becomes legendary and romantic rather than the kind of violence that befell Buck and the victims of the Barrow gang. Were we to be generous, we could say that in its conclusion the film steps out of realism into surrealism, and that because the conclusion is radically different from the rest of the film, except the sequence of Bonnie's meeting with her mother, it succeeds in exalting rather than hurting us. Bonnie and Clyde's bodies meet their destiny in a stunningly dramatic way. Their spirits which, like our spirits, crave absolute freedom, are completely freed; and we all, those of us in the audience, Bonnie and Clyde up there in their glamorous closeups, find somewhere the fulfillment that we cannot find in real life. Together, romantically and mythically, we may be heroes before whom heads are bowed in that great hall somewhere that immortalizes the truly great. And for those of us who do not wish for glory, the end of the film gives a life to self-destructive fantasies.

Youngsters imitate Warren Beatty's mannerisms and Faye Dunaway's look. Bonnie is on the covers of *Life* and *Time*, and models aping her are on fashion-magazine covers. When introduction of the factual aspects of Bonnie and Clyde's crime careers would mar the sheer artistic beauty of the film, they are made unreal. But the executioners of the two are real, revengeful, gross, humorless law-enforcing officials too stupid to comprehend, as C. W. Moss does, that Bonnie and Clyde are special. The sheriff, victimized by pride and sadism, terminates the bodily lives of two beautiful people who had found a beautiful love. Thus the director of the film managed to fashion his subject so that the initiators of violence are the heroes, and the representatives of the law are villains. And the public has bought it—and how!

If *Bonnie and Clyde* had been handled cinematically as tragedy, it might have been a great film. The movie's changing color values and camera speeds would have given the audience the catharsis that is derived from great dramatic works. But the director took a tragic stance without giving us a tragedy. The film slams the audience around until one walks out of the theater feeling bashed in. It is a torturesome emotional experience that leaves one stunned and dissatisfied—some young people have gone back to see it as many as twenty times. But if these same young people met a bona fide tragedy they would be satisfied with less exposure. They would want to analyze and reflect upon rather than re-experience the film. It seems, then, that the director's problem was the same as that encountered when characters in a Broadway musical comedy-drama striving for success have to die or be killed. The "unpleastantness" is rushed by quickly, more production values—lights, costumes, sets —are marshaled on the stage, and a comic character comes immediately to insure that the audience will not have to linger over feelings that might blemish the evening. Thus, Arthur Penn's use of fine artistic devices become, in the context in which he places them, cinematic shenanigans. When used to bail him out of a reality that might be unpleasant, they "put the lie" to his film and expose it as a bag of tawdry tricks.

An apt contrast to *Bonnie and Clyde* is *In Cold Blood*. In this movie, killing kills and violence ends in more violence. No cinematic devices provide an escape valve, making romantic what was not romantic. We experience the film as a tragedy. Dick Hickock and Perry Smith are not pictured through rose-colored glasses. As portrayed by Scott Wilson and Robert Blake, they do not even look like movie actors. They steal, inflict needless cruelty, and murder the whole Clutter family in cold blood. Their actions defy easy comprehension: they are unmotivated, profitless, brutal, and debased.

Except for the cutting, which is at times too slick, and the falsifying and conventional jazz on the sound track early in the film, *In Cold Blood* is an honest, moral, and aesthetically satisfying movie. Richard Brook, its director, attacks his material as an artistic documentarian, and the technical expertness he brings to the film gives it pitch and fever that transform the raw material of history into an object of art. Nothing seems to be dodged. The artistic imagination present in the film takes us to the depths of the horror of the murders and of the execution of the murderers. It stamps us with the theme: killing kills and crime does not pay. Violence is handled much more effectively than in *Bonnie and Clyde,* and the gore is left to the viewer's imagination.

The film is, rightly, in black and white, thus providing a starkness and aesthetic distance that heightens its ability to move into our consciousness. We feel the importance and seriousness of the subject from the very beginning; we know that the film is intended to do something unforgettable to us rather than help us pass an evening. *Bonnie and Clyde,* on the other hand, is rightly in color. Its primary purpose is entertainment, and color joins the viewer to the musical-comedy gaiety and prettiness of the parts of *Oklahoma* that were so effective on the stage. ("Pore" Jud's murder would have been artistically insensitive had it been staged in black and white.) The director of *In Cold Blood,* rather than have us see Perry slash Mr.

Cutter's throat, handles the triple murders in such a way that we get the horrible reality of the facts.

He seems less concerned with having us witness violence than in giving his film a shape and flow that will enable us to progress in comprehension of violence when it comes. The murder sequence comes after we have wallowed in Dick and Perry's sordid and ludicrous lives. Dick and Perry get a grip on us; we care about them and willingly or not, have to see their crime as it really happened. And when we realize that the mind and psyche of a killer are very complex, and perhaps unfathomable, we have to consider it an achievement for a film-maker to take us part of the way.

But an artist's wish and responsibility to create a work that will provide an aesthetic experience is not consummated until members of an audience join him in his creative intent. By his creative act, he saves himself from himself and some of the ravages of his society. His expression gets what is gnawing on him outside of himself so that he can look at it dispassionately. To the extent that he does his work well, is honest, clear, and moral in his execution of it, some in the audience may join him to the point that they save something in themselves and in others. After the dramatic encounter with a work of art, their imaginations may be so charged that they continue to move along a creative road. This is what happens with *In Cold Blood*. A viewer leaves the film having created for himself a better understanding of the ways of life and illnesses that nurture murder. One does not hate Dick and Perry for what they did to the Clutters. One understands what happened to them that made them do it. One realizes that more education, more understanding, and a great ability to delve and discriminate are the most fundamental and certain ways open to us to transform the physiognomy of our violent culture.

"The True Story of Bonnie and Clyde"

Of course, it was an open secret that someone whom Clyde and Bonnie had trusted, had betrayed them. The newspapers were full of it; the town of Arcadia was crawling with rumors to that effect. Officers and Rangers spoke guardedly and gave non-committal answers to reporters. It was not hard to piece the facts together and get the answer.

When we went down after the funeral, some of the country people took us to the house where Clyde and Bonnie were supposed to have lived. Nothing could make me believe that they had lived there. Clyde and Bonnie were so particular about being clean, and this was a filthy hole, with old feed sacks on the floor, and trash and dirt everywhere. There was no glass in the windows and the doors wouldn't close properly. Besides, the house was situated in a spot that was a perfect trap. A single narrow road led down through the pines to it. Clyde Barrow was too clever to have holed himself up in this place, where he could be taken easily and have no chance for flight. Clyde's head worked in times of danger and in times of peace. He always saw to it that there was a good exit. There was no exit here. Just where they did stay is something we don't know, but I'm convinced it was not in this house.

On this morning of May 23, Clyde and Bonnie had driven into town and Bonnie bought a magazine. Probably Clyde purchased supplies. About eight miles out of Gibsland on a little hill, Clyde and Bonnie came upon Henry Methvyn's father. He had stopped his truck and taken the wheel off. He had a puncture, so he said. Clyde parked his car beside the truck and got out to see if he could

From The True Story of Bonnie and Clyde as Told by Bonnie's Mother and Clyde's Sister, *edited by Jan I. Fortune (New York: Signet, 1968), pp. 170–72. Reprinted by permission of Blanche C. Gregory, Inc.*

help. This put the Methvyn truck between Clyde's car and the officers, hidden 100 yards away in the underbrush. Bonnie was sitting in the front seat reading her magazine. For once Clyde's sixth sense wasn't working. He had released Henry Methvyn from Eastham prison farm; Henry had been with him on several robberies and in two gun battles where officers were killed, and therefore Clyde sensed no danger.

Another truck loaded with logs came up the hill and blew the horn for Clyde to move over. Clyde got back in his car and pulled up in front of Mr. Methvyn's truck, and started to back closer. This was what the officers were waiting for. Without a word of warning they all came down with a barrage of machine gun fire. Clyde's last act was to shift the gears into low for a get-away and to reach for his gun.

The first blast from the officers' guns struck Clyde full in the head and the left side. He slumped forward over the wheel. It also ripped Bonnie's body to ribbons and she too fell forward just as the car left the road, careened into a sandbank, and stopped. The officers ran out into the road, still firing. They let loose another blast into the rear and side of the car, in order to make doubly sure. Then they approached the toppled car warily, guns ready to fire again.

Although they had already poured enough lead into both bodies to have killed fifty men, they still doubted that the couple was dead. They were expecting momentarily to hear the rat-tat-tat of returning fire, and to behold Clyde Barrow, the charmed and unkillable, behind the car with a machine gun, ready to fight it out again. But this time there really was no danger.

They reached the car, jerked the door open, and looked inside. A Browning automatic was between Clyde's knees, but his hand had been shot away from his grasp on the weapon. Bonnie, an automatic pistol in her lap, was crumpled over her magazine. Over fifty bullet holes were in each body. They were both quite dead. The long chase was over. The law had won. Bonnie and Clyde would never stand the world off again, two against death, for death had overtaken them at last.

Frank Hamer's Story

On January 16, 1934, between daylight and sunup, four prisoners were delivered from the Eastham Prison Farm, which is a part of the Texas penitentiary system at Huntsville, Texas. One of the guards, Major Crowson, was killed, and four convicts, Joe Palmer, Henry Methvin, Raymond Hamilton, and Hilton Bybee, escaped to an automobile with unknown confederates, who from a concealed position held off the guards with machine-gun fire. It was soon learned that the delivery was planned and executed by Clyde Barrow and one or more companions.

A few weeks later, on April 1, 1934, two state highway patrolmen, E. B. Wheeler and H. D. Murphy, saw a car parked on a side road near Grapevine, Texas, and when they stopped to investigate, or to give aid if needed, they were shot and brutally murdered by a dark-haired man and a red-headed woman. Description by people who saw the couple, together with finger-prints found on a whiskey bottle, indicated that the work was done by Clyde Barrow and Bonnie Parker. These murders brought the total number charged against Barrow to fourteen, shortly raised to fifteen. As a result of these repeated crimes, the whole state was aroused and every peace officer and highway patrolman was on the lookout for the pair.

I was not in the state service, having resigned from the Texas Rangers on November 1, 1932, because Mrs. Miriam A. Ferguson and her husband were soon to take charge—for the fourth time—of the governor's office. About February 1, 1934, Lee Simmons, superintendent of the penitentiary, came to Austin and asked me if I would be willing to take Barrow's trail and follow it to the end. I agreed to try it, and was issued a commission as a state highway patrolman. The fact that I was after Barrow was known to only a few people before we caught him.

From The Texas Rangers *by Walter Prescott Webb (Austin: University of Texas Press, 1965), pp. 539–43. Reprinted by permission of the University of Texas Press.*

On February 10, I took the trail and followed it for exactly 102 days. Like Clyde Barrow I used a Ford V8, and like Clyde I lived in the car most of the time.

I soon had valuable sources of information, but these cannot be revealed without violating confidences. The fact that I never betray a confidence, even from the criminal, has resulted in bringing me inside information which every successful officer must have. I soon learned that Barrow played a circle from Dallas to Joplin, Missouri to Louisiana, and back to Dallas. Occasionally he would leave this beat, but he would always come back to it as most criminals do. One time he and Bonnie went as far east as North Carolina for no other purpose, it seems, than to visit a cigarette factory. Again they would go to Indiana, Iowa, or New Mexico, but like wild horses, they would circle to their old range. The thing to be decided was whether to set the trap in Texas, Missouri, or Louisiana. I decided that Barrow could be most easily caught in Louisiana, because he was "hot" in Texas and in Missouri, having killed men in both states, but he had killed no one in Louisiana, and would probably make that his hiding-place.

It was necessary for me to make a close study of Barrow's habits. I had never seen him, and never saw him until May 23, but I interviewed many people who knew him, and studied the numerous pictures of him and of his woman companion. I knew the size, height, and all the marks of identification of both Clyde and Bonnie. But this was not enough. An officer must know the mental habits of the outlaw, how he thinks, and how he will act in different situations. When I began to understand Clyde Barrow's mind, I felt that I was making progress. I learned that Barrow never holed up at one place; he was always on the go; and he traveled farther in one day than any fugitive that I have ever followed. He thought nothing of driving a thousand miles at a stretch. Barrow was also a master of side roads, which made his movements irregular. Around Dallas, Joplin, and in Louisiana, he seemed to know them all.

Before the chase ended, I not only knew the general appearance and mental habits of the pair, but I had learned the kind of whiskey they drank, what they ate, and the color, size, and texture of their clothes. I first struck their trail at Texarkana. At Logansport they bought a half-gallon of whiskey; near Keechi they bought gasoline, and then went in the night to a negro house and had the negroes cook them some cornbread and fry a chicken. In Shreveport they bought pants, underwear, gloves, and an automatic shotgun. In their camp on the Wichita River, near Wichita Falls, they lost or threw away some bills for goods bought in Dallas. From the clerk I learned the size, color, and pattern of one of Bonnie's dresses, and the kind of ascot tie and belt buckle she wore. A description of these was sent to Ed Portley of Joplin, Missouri, with information that Clyde and Bonnie were probably hiding in some abandoned mines near by.

But the trail always led back to Louisiana, where I located their hideout on February 17. I cannot give the name of the parish because of what followed. Because I was out of Texas, it was desirable for me to take the local officers into my confidence. I learned that the sheriff of this parish could not be trusted, and so it was arranged to have Barrow's hideout moved into a parish where the officers were more reliable. In a comparatively short time the hideout was established in Bienville Parish at a place well known to me.

The next task was to catch Clyde when he was "at home." On several occasions I went alone to this secret place. It was my hope to take him and Bonnie alive; this I could do only by finding them asleep. It would have been simple to tap each one on the head, kick their weapons out of reach, and handcuff them before they knew what it was all about. Once the plan came near succeeding, and would have succeeded but for one of those accidents which will happen over which the officer has no control. There was always plenty of sign in the camp: stubs of Bonnie's Camels—Clyde smoked Bull Durham—lettuce leaves for the white rabbit, pieces of sandwiches, and a button off Clyde's coat. I found where they had made their bed.

The end would have come two or three weeks earlier had not some local and federal officers made a drag on Ruston, Louisiana, and when Clyde heard of it, he quit the country and I had to wait for him to return.

I traveled alone until shortly before the middle of April. On April 10, I called Chief L. G. Phares of the Highway Patrol to tell him that Barrow had used a Pontiac sedan to make his getaway after killing Constable Cummings and kidnaping the chief of police of Commerce, Oklahoma. I gave Chief Phares the license and engine number of this car and also the numbers on extra license plates from Oklahoma and Louisiana which Clyde carried in his car. Chief Phares told me that the Highway Department had decided to hire an

extra man to travel with me. I asked for B. M. Gault who had served
with me in the Headquarters Ranger Company. Gault met me in
Dallas on April 14, and traveled with me until the chase ended on
May 28.

Bob Alcorn and Ted Hinton, from the sheriff's department of
Dallas, gave me information, and were members of the party that met
Barrow. In Louisiana I made contact with Sheriff Henderson Jordan
of Bienville Parish, and after I had informed him of my plan, he
agreed to assist me and pay no attention to other officers, state or
federal. He brought with him Deputy Oakley.

We did not find Barrow in his hideout but at his "post office."
All criminals who work in groups must have some way of communicating with one another when they get separated. I learned
that Clyde had his post office on a side road about eight miles from
Plain Dealing, Louisiana. It was under a board which lay on the
ground near a large stump of a pine tree. The point selected was
on a knoll from which Bonnie in the car could command a view
of the road while Clyde went into the forest for his mail.

By the night of May 22, we had good reason to believe that Clyde
would visit this mail box within a short time. About midnight we
drove out of Gibsland, secreted our cars in the pines, and made
arrangements to furnish him more news than he had ever received
at one time. No detail was neglected. The road here runs north and
south, and the knoll over which it rises is made by a spur or point
which slopes from east to west. The stump that marked the location
of the post office is on the west side of the road. We therefore took
our position on the opposite, and higher, side so that we could look
down on the car and its occupants. Within an hour after we reached
the place, which was about 2.30 in the morning, we had constructed
a blind from pine branches within about twenty-five or thirty feet of
the point where the car would stop.

We expected Barrow to come from the north, or from our right as
we faced the road. The six men were spaced at intervals of about
ten feet, parallel to the road. I held the position on the extreme left,
and next was Gault, Jordan, Alcorn, Oakley, and Hinton in the
order named. Gault, Jordan, and myself were to take care of the
front seat, Oakley and Alcorn of the back seat, if occupied, while
Ted Hinton at the end of the line represented the reserves. If the
car got past us, Hinton was to step out and bust the engine with a

Browning Machine Gun. Jordan and I had automatic shot guns, three had Winchesters, one a machine gun, and all carried revolvers or automatic pistols.

We agreed to take Barrow and the woman alive if we could. We believed that when they stopped the car, both would be looking towards the post office and away from us; such action on their part would enable us to escape observation until we demanded their surrender.

With everything ready, we had nothing to do but wait about seven hours, without breakfast or coffee. Waiting is about the hardest thing an officer has to do. Many men will stand up in a fight, but lose their nerve completely if required to wait long for the excitement. On this occasion I did not detect the slightest nervousness on the part of a single man.

As daylight came a few cars passed, and occasionally a logger's truck; and the sun came up at our back, which was in our favor. It was probably about 9.10 when we heard a humming through the pines that was different from that made by the other motors. A car was coming from the north at a terrific speed, singing like a sewing machine. We heard it when it must have been three miles away.

Finally, it came into view at a distance of a thousand yards, and though it was still coming rapidly, it began to slow down as it climbed the hill towards us. We first recognized the color of the car, a gray Ford sedan, then the license number; we saw two persons, a small black-headed man and a small red-haired woman. We recognized Clyde and Bonnie, and knew there was no mistake. The speed continued to slacken under the brakes and the car came to a full stop at the exact spot that we had previously decided it would.

When Barrow brought the car to a standstill, he pressed the clutch and slipped into low gear with the engine idling. Just as we had figured, both he and the woman peered with all their attention towards the stump.

At the command, "stick 'em up!" both turned, but instead of obeying the order as we had hoped, they clutched the weapons which they either held in their hands or in their laps. When the firing began, Barrow's foot released the clutch and the car, in low gear, moved forward on the decline and turned into the ditch on the left. I looked at my watch and it was 9.20.

There can be no question raised as to who fired the first or the fatal shots. All fired as we had agreed to do and every man in the squad did everything that he was supposed to do. It was not a pleasant duty, but it was a duty which no one shirked. Should I ever go on such another case, I hope that I shall have the help of such men as the five who were with me that day.

An examination of the car revealed that the shots had been accurately placed, most of them ranging from the position of the driver's feet upwards at an angle that would take into account the entire body. The examination also revealed that the car was nothing but an arsenal on wheels. The inventory included:

3	Browning automatic rifles	Cal.	30
1	sawed-off shotgun	Gauge	20
1	sawed-off shotgun	Gauge	16
1	Colt automatic pistol	Cal.	32
1	Colt automatic pistol	Cal.	380
1	Colt revolver, double action	Cal.	45
7	Colt automatic pistols	Cal.	45
100	machine gun clips of 20 cartridges each.		
3000	rounds of ammunition scattered all over the car.		

As soon as possible, I called Chief Phares at Austin and told him that the job was done.

"Barrow and Woman Are Slain by Police in Louisiana Trap"

ARCADIA, La., May 23.—Fifty bullets from the guns of old time Texas rangers and country Sheriffs today ended the murderous career of Clyde Barrow and his blond gunwoman, Bonnie Parker. They drove their small sedan into the trap and six officers pumped 167 bullets into the car.

Fifty shots struck the bandits before they could raise their guns. Mortally wounded, Barrow kicked open the door of the car and attempted to fire at the officers, but death overtook him before he could pull the trigger. He died with a gun in his hands without saying a word.

Bonnie Parker died with her head between her knees with a machine gun across her lap. She was famous as a cigar-smoking woman, but when she died she clutched a package of blood-soaked cigarettes in her left hand. Fingers of her right hand, the trigger hand which was her proud boast, were shot away by the officers' bullets.

The trail of the bandit pair was ended through the cunning of Frank Hamer, who, with three Texans, had trailed the bandit couple over a half dozen States for 15,000 miles. He was rewarded for his search through a ruse accomplished by the aid of the father of an ex-convict on the promise that the convict, who had broken prison, would receive consideration from the law.

Barrow and the Parker woman were led to believe they were among friends but their trust led them to their deaths. They were

From The New York Times, *May 24, 1934. Copyright, 1934, by the Associated Press. Reprinted by permission of The New York Times Company and the Associated Press.*

taken by surprise and were unable to use the many guns and pistols they carried in the car at arm's reach.

The officers gave the bandits the same medicine they had meted out to their victims in more than a dozen fights and raids against the law in which twelve men were killed. In many of the fights Bonnie Parker, forgetting her convict husband, stood side by side with her outlaw associate and shot it out with the officers, each time successfully, until today.

When the officers ceased fire and approached the car, they found Barrow full of bullets slumped against the steering wheel with his head hanging out of the window. Bonnie Parker was slumped forward beside him, dead from many bullets. With the bodies lying just as they were, the car was towed to Arcadia where an inquest was held. The bodies were then put on public exhibition until they were claimed by relatives, who took them to Dallas for burial.

Bonnie Parker was identified by a tattoo on the thigh. She wore diamond rings, an expensive wrist watch and a holy cross around her neck under her dress. She was clad in a red dress, red shoes and a red and white hat.

Barrow had $507 on his person and was wearing colored glasses, one lens of which was shot out. He was identified positively by a missing big toe on his left foot.

The car held a regular arsenal and several blankets, leaving the impression that the pair frequently had slept in the car. Automobile licenses from a dozen States were found in the automobile, which was almost new. It bore a 1934 Arkansas license plate.

Hamer, a big strapping Texan, gave his comrades credit for bringing down the pair and expressed regret over having to kill a woman.

"I hate to bust a cap on a woman," he said, "especially when she was sitting down. However, if it hadn't been her, it would have been us."

Although inseparable in crime, Bonnie Parker and Clyde Barrow have been separated in death by Barrow's mother, who objected to double funeral services for the pair in Dallas. She said she would demand a separate funeral service for her boy.

The incongruity of the criminal mind was demonstrated by discovery that Clyde Barrow while not toying with machine guns and revolvers was a saxophone player. Nestled between guns and ammunition, a saxophone, with several pieces of sheet music, was found in the automobile.

On the floor under the front seat a partially eaten sandwich was found, indicating that Bonnie was eating the sandwich at the time of the officers' attack.

"Barrow's Killings Date from Parole"

Clyde Barrow was a snake-eyed murderer who killed without giving his victims a chance to draw. He was slight, altogether unheroic in physical appearance.

Bonnie Parker was a fit companion for him. She was a hard-faced, sharp-mouthed woman who gave up a waitress job in a Kansas City restaurant to become the mistress of Ray Hamilton, Texas bank robber. Barrow took her away from Hamilton.

There were two Barrow brothers, Clyde and Marvin Ivan, who bore the nicknames Buck and Ivy. Both, like John Dillinger, were released on parole and from then on ran wild over the Southwest, killing right and left.

The number of deaths attributed to Dillinger and his band after he was paroled totals about thirteen. The Barrows and the Parker woman, when they were turned loose on parole, murdered about twelve persons. The exact number is uncertain. Eight of their victims were policemen or guards.

The Barrows were sons of Harry Barrow, owner of a gasoline station in West Dallas. They began a career of petty crime in San Antonio and Dallas while they were still in their teens, but escaped conviction until 1930. They were "investigated" in a number of motorcar thefts, but managed to squirm out of trouble each time.

FIRST SENTENCED IN 1930

Early in January, four years ago, they were picked up in a stolen car in Henrietta, Texas. Marvin was sentenced to four years in Huntsville prison and Clyde, who had confessed not only to the

From The New York Times, *May 24, 1934.* © *1934 by The New York Times Company. Reprinted by permission.*

car theft but to two burglaries, pleaded guilty and received a two-year sentence.

On March 8, 1930, Marvin, then a "trusty" or privileged prisoner, walked out of the jail and three days later smuggled saws into Clyde's cell. Clyde cut his way out that night, taking two companions with him.

His freedom was short-lived. He was picked up in Middletown, Ohio, a week later and re-entered Huntsville under a longer sentence. With penalties for the jail break he was supposed to serve fourteen years, but he walked free on Feb. 2, 1932 on a general parole signed by the Governor.

Marvin Barrow, meanwhile, had returned to prison of his own volition. Two days after Christmas, 1931, he surrendered. He had married after his escape, and his wife, Blanche Caldwell, had persuaded him to go back, he said.

A month after Clyde got out on parole he was identified as a member of a band of filling-station looters. That was the limit of his ambition, it seemed. None of his robberies ever netted him and his followers more than $3,500.

His homicidal career started two months after he was paroled. In Hillsboro, Texas, late on the night of April 27, 1932, he awakened John Bucher, a merchant, on the pretense that he wanted to buy guitar strings. Another man was with him. When Bucher turned his back they shot him. Their loot was $40 in cash.

Five months later, at a dance hall in Atoka, Okla., Sheriff C. G. Maxwell and Eugene Moore, under-sheriff, saw two young men—strangers in town—drinking out of a bottle. Maxwell told them to put the bottle away.

"We don't permit that here," he said.

"Oh, you don't?"

Out came a revolver. Moore was shot through the heart. Maxwell fell dangerously wounded. The strangers—Clyde Barrow and Ray Hamilton—leaped into their stolen car and got away. They never gave their victims a chance to draw.

At Grand Prairie, Texas, not long afterward, Clyde Barrow's band staged its hold-up masterpiece—a $3,500 raid on the interurban station in the town. They drifted on, in stolen automobiles, while Rangers, highway patrols and town police searched in vain for them on the roads.

They showed up again in the Fall, this time at Sherman, Texas.

On Oct. 11 they entered a butcher shop owned by Howard Hall, 70 years old. They poked revolvers at Hall and Homer Glaze, a clerk. Hall tried to push the weapon away. They shot him in the abdomen and left him, dead.

Doyle Johnson, a citizen of Temple, Texas, tried to prevent a young man and a young woman from stealing his car in front of his home, one night in December, 1932. They shot him off the running board of the car as they drove away. That, it turned out later, was the first appearance of Bonnie Parker in the picture.

Clyde Barrow had met her in the Kansas City restaurant. Ray Hamilton, her man, was serving a long sentence for robbery at the time. He had been picked up after the shooting in Atoka. He had quarreled with Barrow over Bonnie and they had gone separate ways.

List of Killings Grows

Malcolm Davis, a deputy, was shot to death by Barrow at Fort Worth when he approached the murderer's stolen car to inspect the license plates. He got no warning, no chance to draw. A volley of shotgun-slugs killed him. That was on Jan. 7, 1933.

Sergeant G. B. Kahler of the State Highway Patrol in Joplin, Mo., and a raiding party located Barrow, the Parker woman, Marvin Barrow and his wife, in a stone house that had living quarters on the upper floor and a garage in the lower floor. It was the morning of April 18.

The garage doors suddenly burst open, a car shot out, its occupants spraying machine gun bullets from both sides. Constable J. W. Harryman and Detective Harry L. McGinnis fell in the road, mortally wounded. When the troopers entered the house they found Marvin Barrow's parole certificate and some cigar stubs marked with the imprint of tiny teeth, Bonnie Parker's signature.

At Alma, Ark., on June 23, Clyde Barrow killed Henry Humphrey, a city marshal who tried to prevent a general-store hold-up, and got away again. Posses roamed the countryside, but the Barrows were elusive. They fled to the woods and lived on canned goods, afraid to venture into a town or village.

In the running fight with a posse outside of Platte City, Mo., the Barrows and Bonnie Parker wounded three policemen and got away.

Five days later, on July 24, they were surrounded in a woods near Dexter, Iowa. They fought from behind a barricade formed by a fallen tree.

Marvin Barrow was hit three times in that fight. He and his wife were picked up by the attacking party after Clyde and Bonnie Parker had fled. The fugitives waded a stream, ran through a corn field to a farmhouse, stole the farmer's car and escaped. Marvin Barrow died soon afterward in an Iowa hospital. His wife was sent to the penitentiary under a ten-year sentence.

Another six months passed before Clyde Barrow turned up again, this time at the prison from which he had been paroled. He had hidden three revolvers in a clump of weeds on the prison farm and had sent a letter to Ray Hamilton, describing their location. A short distance from the farm, hidden by trees, he had a fast car, with Bonnie Parker at the wheel.

Hamilton and four other convicts, who knew of the plan, reached the hidden pistols. They killed Major Crowson, one of the guards, and wounded Olan Bozeman, another. Then they headed for the automobile, Barrow covering their retreat with a steady stream of machine gun fire. He and the gun were concealed in a bushy undergrowth. Bonnie Parker kept tooting the horn to guide them. They gained the car and got away.

Gabe Wright, a Negro, captured J. B. French, a "lifer," one of the four who escaped with Hamilton, when French entered his cabin the next day. All the others, including Hamilton, were picked up, one by one, but not before they had done further damage.

At Grapevine, Texas, on the morning of April 2, 1934, State Highway Patrolmen E. B. Wheeler and H. D. Murphy were passing a car parked in the road when, without warning, machine guns mowed them down. Clyde Barrow's finger prints were found on a whiskey bottle at the spot. And there were some cigar butts with tiny tooth marks beside the bottle.

The last murder attributed to Clyde Barrow and Bonnie Parker was committed in Miami, Okla., on April 6. Cal Campbell, a 63-year-old constable, was shot to death and Percy Boyd, police chief, was shot in the face as they approached Barrow's car, which was mired in the mud. The murderers stole a farmer's car to get away.

Clyde Barrow was heard from again when Hamilton went on trial in Texas following his capture in Sherman, in that State. He sent a mocking letter to the authorities, in which he scoffed at Hamilton for a published statement that he (Barrow) was the instigator of all the killings. Hamilton was sentenced to 362 years in prison.

That was a month ago. He eluded his pursuers until yesterday.

Changes and Revisions from Original Script to Film

Episode no.	Film	Original Script
1	Title sequences	See above, pp. 56–59, for discussion of changes in titles.
2	Meeting of Bonnie and Clyde.	Almost unchanged from OS.
3	First grocery-store robbery.	Same in original script.
4	First escape and love scene: Bonnie and Clyde steal a car. Bonnie tries to seduce Clyde. Clyde reveals his impotence, but persuades Bonnie to join his career of crime anyway.	Although this episode is basically the same in original script, there is considerable revision. Clyde's impotence and his shame about it much more explicit in film than in original script. Penn apparently wants characters to disturb and challenge each other more.
6	Bonnie and Clyde stop at café, and then steal another car to continue their flight.	Some changes in dialogue here, mainly to speed up action.
7	Bonnie and Clyde wake up at deserted farmhouse. Clyde teaches Bonnie to shoot. Farmer and his old Negro hand come along and shoot out windows.	In original script, there is a long scene of Clyde teaching Bonnie to shoot that is largely cut. Also, the farmer is from elsewhere and does not shoot. There is no old Negro in original script. In the film, Penn emphasizes the wider social context of the depression more explicitly than in original script.
8	First bank robbery.	Same as original script.
9	Second grocery-store robbery.	Important changes in Clyde's reaction after the robbery: in original

138

Epi-sode no.	Film	Original Script
		script Clyde's main response to debacle of robbery is to decide he needs a larger gang; in film, he is horrified at the violence of the butcher.
10	Meeting with C. W. Moss.	In original script, the meeting with C. W. is more purposive, since Bonnie and Clyde are looking for a gang member. In the film, it is the accidental result of engine trouble. A number of speeches in original script that made Bonnie more of a wise-cracking flapper are cut.
11	Wounded butcher looking at photographs.	Two scenes from original script were cut out at this point: a scene in a motel with the three characters sleeping in one room and Bonnie looking frustrated; another in a cafe where C. W. puts sugar on everything to the disgust of the other two characters.
12	Second bank robbery in which the elderly teller is shot.	Same as original script.
13	Escape and scene in movie theater.	In original script, there is a scene in the escaping car where Clyde angrily chews out C. W. and then discusses getting his brother Buck to join the gang. In the film, the scene shifts almost immediately to the movie house.
14	First motel scene.	An important scene in original script involving sexual teasing between Bonnie and C. W. was cut entirely from the film, presumably because of the sexual perversity it implied between Bonnie and Clyde. Instead, the scene begins with a gesture of love between Bonnie and

Clyde, Clyde telling Bonnie that she can get away since the police don't know who she is, and Bonnie determining to stay with Clyde.

The love scene that follows has important differences between original script and the film. Original script has love-making begin and become very passionate. Then Bonnie pushes a gun off the bed and Clyde grabs for it. "The meaning of his choice is clear to Bonnie at this heightened moment." Bonnie grabs the gun from Clyde and they fight. Clyde is sexually aroused but then overwhelmed by Bonnie's aggression. He rejects her—"Clyde turns away anguished at his failure and ashamed." Bonnie starts in the direction of C. W., and then goes out the front door. Clyde picks up his gun and starts twirling it as we dissolve to the next episode.

In the film, Clyde feels deeply touched after Bonnie refuses to leave him. They embrace and the guns fall to the floor. Then Clyde breaks off the embrace. Bonnie embraces him from behind, and then lets go and returns to bed. Bonnie smiles at Clyde. "She is moved and pained for him. She touches her cheek with the gun and waits for him to be able to look at her. Her look eases him."

In general, guns have very different meanings in original script and in the film. In original script they are actively sexual: a symbolic substitute for real sexuality.

Epi-sode no.	*Film*	*Original Script*
		In the film, the symbolic aspect of the guns, while present, is less explicitly stressed. They are more part of the furniture.
15	Arrival of Buck and Blanche and departure for Joplin.	Original script had a much more extended treatment of the introduction of Buck and Blanche, presumably cut because it unnecessarily slowed down the action. Instead, a new scene between Buck and Clyde in the motel room was added in which they discuss the murder Clyde committed and Buck asks for assurance that he had to do it. The scene is important in suggesting a rudimentary moral code and in showing the still boyish sense of life controlling the attitudes of Buck and Clyde.
16	Joplin gun battle.	Only minor changes from original script.
17	Reaction after the battle.	Considerably changed from original script. Original script confrontation of Buck and Clyde ending in fight in which Buck knocks Clyde down and then accepts the situation. In the film, this is changed to a scene between Bonnie and Clyde. They argue about Blanche and then make up.
18	Scene in car with reading of newspaper.	Original script emphasizes the newspaper report of the Joplin battle. In the film, the newspaper account deals with many Barrow crimes, emphasizing the myth-making theme.
19	Capture and taunting of Frank Hamer.	The many important changes in this episode are discussed in the essay above, pp. 74–76. Original

Epi-sode no.	*Film*	*Original Script*
20	Third bank robbery.	script has a scene, cut from the film, of the characters getting dressed for the next robbery. With minor changes, the robbery is the same as in original script.

At this point, the film departs substantially from the original script, which proceeds as follows: (21) A scene in the car erupts into an argument between Bonnie and Blanche, followed by Bonnie's running away (cf. episode 23 in the film); (22) the scene of the family picnic; (23) a brief scene after the picnic when Bonnie comes upon the sleeping C. W. and sees his bare chest, thus motivating (24) a tattoo parlor scene in which Bonnie helps C. W. select a design for a tattoo, with much emphasis on Bonnie's pathetic urge for decorative expression; (25) a humorous scene in which Buck holds up a hamburger stand, folksy comedy of the gangsters as ordinary people; (26) a scene at a dry-cleaner's. After Clyde and Buck pick up their cleaning, they come upon two children playing Bonnie and Clyde. Buck laughs at Clyde's embarrassment then is himself put on the spot when the kids don't know who Buck Barrow is; (27) the distribution of the take, with argument about Blanche's share; (28) the kidnapping of Eugene and Velma; (29) The Platte City gun battle. At this point, the film returns to the order of the original script.

A comparison of this section of the film with the original script shows that Penn made two major readjustments. First, he eliminated a number of short scenes, such as the dry-cleaning shop, the hamburger-stand robbery, the tattoo parlor, etc., which not only confused and watered down the sense of dramatic progression, but also tended to cast a slightly perverse and ridiculous light on the protagonists. By eliminating these scenes, Penn not only intensified the action, but emphasized its increasingly tragic implications. Second, by transposing the family picnic scene and the kidnapping of Eugene and Velma, Penn gave a stronger motivation to the former scene and made it more emphatically a part of Bonnie's and the audience's sense of the gang's increasing isolation and doom.

21	Distribution of money after the third bank robbery.	In the film, this scene is directly connected with the third bank robbery and, by emphasizing the small amount of money gained, immediately deflates the gang's successful accomplishment of the robbery. The succeeding argument about

Episode no.	Film	Original Script
		Blanche's share is approximately the same as in original script.
22	Kidnapping of Eugene and Velma.	Same as original script with minor changes in dialogue.
23	Bonnie's flight.	In original script, there is much more emphasis in this scene on the bitter quarrel with Blanche. In the film, the scene expresses Bonnie's general sense of impending doom and her desire to see her mother one last time, thus leading up to family picnic episode.
24	Family picnic.	Very pointed dialogue stressing the gang's impending doom added to scene as presented in original script.
25	Gunfight at Platte City motel.	Important scene between Bonnie and Clyde before the gunfight added in the film. This scene expressed Bonnie's overwhelming despair and Clyde's tenderness toward her.
		A very curious scene was added in the shooting script in which Bonnie and Clyde play dead by dressing up in funeral clothes, assuming coffin positions and singing, "The worms crawl in, the worms crawl out. . . ." Although striking in a macabre way, this scene would have completely disrupted the sense of tenderness in despair between the two protagonists expressed earlier in the episode; it was cut in the film. The gunfight itself is almost exactly as described in original script.
26	Battle at Dexter, Iowa, with death of Buck, capture of Blanche, and wounding of Bonnie and Clyde.	Basically the same as original script.

Episode no.	Film	Original Script
27	The Okie camp: C. W. stops for food and water. Okies regard wounded Bonnie and Clyde with awe.	Same as original script, with minor changes.
28	Arrival at the Moss farm.	Same as original script.
29	Scene in sheriff's office with arrival of Frank Hamer.	Considerably shorter in film than in original script.
30	The Moss farm: Bonnie and Clyde with Moss on the porch; C. W. and his father argue in the kitchen.	These scenes changed from original script, but the major dramatic points are the same.
31	In the hospital: Hamer questions Blanche with false sympathy and gets the name of Moss from her.	In original script, the scene in which Bonnie reads her ballad to Clyde precedes the scene between Hamer and Blanche. In the film, the reading of the poem and the subsequent love between the protagonists is ironically qualified by our knowledge that their hiding place will soon be known.
32	Bonnie reads her poem to Clyde and they finally consummate their love.	

There are major differences between this scene in original script and in the film, corresponding to Penn's attempt to achieve a more tragic emotion in the doom of the protagonists. In original script, when Bonnie finishes reading her poem, the camera cuts to Clyde who is twirling his gun (cf., the phallic symbolism noted in connection with episode 14). In the conversation that follows, Clyde continues twirling his gun and remarks that he wishes Buck could hear the poem. Bonnie gets a bit angry at this. After a tense silence, Clyde says that, after all, Buck was family. Bonnie tartly replies that she is family too, and then gets angrily out of the car. Clyde continues to twirl his gun. Finally, Bonnie gets up on the hood of the car and begins to twirl her gun in perfect synchronization with his. Clyde begins to laugh and Bonnie "slowly starts to smile." Original script then cuts to the hospital and the Blanche-Hamer scene.

In the film, this episode becomes the authentic consummation of Bonnie and Clyde's love, rather than a final expression of their perverted erotic-aggressive relationship. When Bonnie finishes reading her poem, we see a closeup of Clyde saying in gleeful wonder, "Damn! That's me." At last, Clyde feels that he has achieved some fulfillment, that he has become the stuff of legend. Bonnie also laughs joyfully. Laughing together, they begin to make love. But at this point, a scene between Hamer and old Moss is intercut. Whereas in original script, the betrayal scene is done with considerable dialogue between Hamer and Moss, in the film this scene is done quickly, with visuals alone, thus ironically commenting on Bonnie and Clyde's successful intercourse. After seeing Hamer and Moss, we return to Bonnie and Clyde. Their love-making finished, they are terrifically happy. The effect is of exuberant innocence and the sudden breakthrough of normal erotic feelings. Clyde asks Bonnie if his lovemaking was all right and she replies that it was perfect.

Episode no.	Film	Original Script
33	Conversation between C. W. and his father at the farm. Moss tells C. W. not to be with Bonnie and Clyde.	Basically the same as original script though a number of these short final scenes are rearranged and some are eliminated to make the final action go faster.
34	Bonnie and Clyde in the bedroom at the farm.	Same dialogue as original script, but the preceding love scene makes Clyde's inability to imagine any alternative way of life more ironic and fateful.
35	Bonnie and Clyde in town. They miss C. W., and are forced to leave town because of arrival of police car.	Same as original script though some minor changes are made, such as the arrival of the police car to motivate Bonnie and Clyde's departure.
36	Final ambush.	This scene and some of the major changes from original script are discussed above, pp. 79–83.

Plot Synopsis

The story begins, one bright spring day, with Bonnie Parker, who is sitting in her room, bitterly unhappy about the narrowness and dullness of her life as a waitress in a cheap café. Her attention is attracted by a young man who has come into the yard, apparently to steal her mother's car. Bonnie calls to him, and then goes down to talk with him, drawn by a strong feeling of excitement. The two walk into town, and the young man, Clyde Barrow, brags to Bonnie about his daring, his prison sentence, and his gun. Taunted by Bonnie, Clyde finally holds up a grocery store to prove his courage and power, and the two escape in a stolen car. Terrifically aroused by Clyde and the robbery, Bonnie throws herself at him physically, but discovers that Clyde is impotent. Clyde appeals to Bonnie's need for excitement and affection, however, and she agrees to join him as a partner in crime.

After two rather confused and ineffective robberies, Bonnie and Clyde team up with C. W. Moss, a rather stupid but hero-worshipping country boy; with C. W. driving, they successfully rob a bank, but are forced to kill a pursuing teller when C. W. stupidly gets the escape car momentarily pinned into a parking place. From this point on, the Barrow gang is the object of a widespread search. After meeting Clyde's brother Buck and his wife Blanche, they try to hide out in Joplin, Missouri, but the police find out and attempt to capture them. During their narrow escape from the Joplin trap, they killed policemen, marking themselves for destruction. Shortly after the Joplin escape, they encounter for the first time the man who will become their nemesis, Texas Ranger Frank Hamer.

For a time, the gang is successful in evading its pursuers and even enjoys its hunted celebrity, following stories of its exploits in the newspapers. Yet the increasing pressures of flight cause tensions within the gang to erupt from time to time, particularly the hostility between Bonnie and Blanche. Although Bonnie's increasing awareness that the gang's criminal career is just another destructive trap leads her to try to run away, her increasing sense of doom brings her closer to Clyde. After a desperate but hopeless attempt to recapture the feeling of Bonnie's old life by attending a family picnic, Bonnie and Clyde realize they have nothing left but each other.

From this point, their pursuers move ever closer. Surrounded by police at a motel in Platte City, the gang escapes from the night attack but is trapped again at dawn in a field outside Dexter, Iowa. Buck Barrow is killed, Blanche captured, and Bonnie and Clyde both seriously wounded. Only the greatest luck enables C. W. to help them escape to his father's farm near Arcadia, Louisiana. While recovering at the farm, Bonnie reads her ballad "The Story of Bonnie and Clyde" to Clyde, and they are finally able to consummate their love. Ironically, just as Bonnie and Clyde discover how to fulfill themselves in love rather than in robbery and violence, they are betrayed to the police by C. W. Moss's father.

Lured into an ambush on their way back to the farm from Arcadia, they die in a terrible hail of bullets.

Content Outline

I. THE MEETING OF BONNIE AND CLYDE

Bonnie in her room alone. Clyde appears in yard intending to steal car. Bonnie comes down.

Camera tracks them into town. They talk while having cokes at gas station.

First robbery (grocery store). Flight in stolen car.

Bonnie, sexually aroused, tries to make love to Clyde, forcing him to reveal his impotence. Having stopped car they talk in grove of trees and then in café, Clyde persuading Bonnie to join him in career of crime.

At deserted farmhouse where they have slept, Clyde shows Bonnie how to fire gun, and then talks with dispossessed farmer and his Black tenant; they shoot out windows of house as gesture of anger against the bankers.

First bank robbery; the bank turns out to have failed several days earlier.

Second grocery store robbery; Clyde is attacked by butcher, whom he shoots.

II. THE GATHERING OF THE GANG

Meeting with C. W. Moss at gas station where he works; Bonnie and Clyde persuade C. W. to join them.

Second bank robbery; C. W. parks car and then can't get out when Bonnie and Clyde come running out; elderly teller jumps on running board and is shot by panic-stricken Clyde.

Movie theater: after their escape, the trio go to movie theater, where "Golddiggers of 1933" is playing; Clyde bitterly blames C. W. for the murder; Bonnie is engrossed by movie.

In motel, Bonnie and Clyde attempt to make love, but Clyde

cannot overcome his impotence. Scene reveals developing tenderness and love toward each other.

Meeting with Buck Barrow and his wife Blanche.

III. THE TRIUMPH OF THE GANG

Gun battle at Joplin and successful escape from police ambush. Capture and taunting of Frank Hamer.

Third bank robbery: the gang reaches its highpoint in this successfully organized robbery; the escape is one of the wildest moments of almost-slapstick comedy in the film.

IV. THE BREAKING UP OF THE GANG

By the roadside, after the third bank robbery, the gang argues about the distribution of the spoils; quarrel between Bonnie and Blanche erupts and is halted by discovery that car is leaking oil.

Seeking another car, the gang steals one belonging to undertaker Eugene Grizzard and his girlfriend Velma; Eugene and Velma pursue and are in turn chased and taken for a ride by the gang, who desperately feel the need for some kind of human companionship.

Shortly after this episode, perhaps the next morning, Bonnie decides to run away; she is chased through a cornfield by Clyde and she tells him of her need to see her mother.

The family picnic: shot in soft focus and with a skillful use of montage to suggest how impossible it has become for Bonnie and Clyde to establish any kind of ordinary family life; scene ends with ominous interchange between Clyde and Bonnie's mother.

Gunfight at the Platte City Motel: episode opens with tender scene between Bonnie and Clyde at the motel; Blanche and C. W. go out for fried chicken and are seen by deputy sheriff; police surround motel with armored car and many men, and then attack; the gang escapes but Buck and Blanche are wounded; this episode leads immediately to the next.

Battle at Dexter, Iowa: as dawn comes up we see the gang in

the middle of a field surrounded by men with guns; Buck is badly wounded; they desperately try to escape, but their cars are shot to pieces; shot several more times, Buck dies; Blanche is captured; Bonnie, C. W., and Clyde escape across a river, but Bonnie and Clyde are both wounded in the process.

V. THE DESTRUCTION OF BONNIE AND CLYDE

The Okie camp: driving Bonnie and Clyde away from the Dexter battle, C. W. stops for water and food at a camp of dispossessed farmers; the farmers, discovering who they are, treat the badly wounded Bonnie and Clyde with a reverential awe.

Arrival at Moss farm: at the end of the flight, Bonnie and Clyde are taken to the farm of C. W. Moss's father.

Frank Hamer arrives at Dexter in the wake of the battle.

Bonnie and Clyde are shown convalescing at the Moss farm; Clyde is angry at newspaper reports that he deserted his brother; later, C. W. and his father have an argument in the kitchen about his tattoo; the scene prepares us for the treachery of C. W.'s father.

Frank Hamer questions Blanche and discovers the name of C. W. Moss, thereby giving him a clue to Bonnie and Clyde's whereabouts.

Bonnie reads her poem to Clyde, and, at last, they are able to make love; their lovemaking is ironically intercut with a scene of Hamer meeting C. W.'s father in the nearby town of Arcadia and making a deal with him for the ambush of Bonnie and Clyde.

C. W.'s father tells him to elude Bonnie and Clyde when they go to Arcadia the next day; C. W. states his conviction that no lawman can catch Bonnie and Clyde.

In Arcadia, Bonnie shows Clyde the little china figurine of a shepherdess she has purchased; seeing a police car, and unable to locate C. W., they start back for the farm.

Ambush and death of Bonnie and Clyde.

Script Extract

I. The Opening Sequences (final-script version)

The film begins with TWO TITLE CARDS introducing the central characters, executed in the style of similar cards used to begin the serials of the late 1930's. The title cards show a photograph of the character looking straight ahead, posed against the plain white background. The words appear at the bottom of the frame. The frame should be smaller than 1: 85–1.

Title Card 1:

BONNIE PARKER, who was born in Rowena, Texas, 1910, and moved with her large family to West Dallas. In 1931 she worked as a waitress in a cafe before meeting Clyde Barrow and beginning her career in crime.

Title Card 2:

CLYDE BARROW, who was born in Telco, Texas, 1909, to a family of sharecroppers. As a young man he became a small-time thief and was apprehended after robbing a gas station. He served two years in the penitentiary for armed robbery and was released on good behavior in 1931.

Credits: Bonnie and Clyde

CREDITS should be simple and absolutely silent. No music should occur in the film until where first indicated in the script.

FADE IN:

1. *Int. Bedroom*   *Closeup of Bonnie Parker*   *Day*

Blonde, somewhat fragile, intelligent in expression. She is putting on make-up with intense concentration and appreciation, applying lipstick and eye make-up. As the CAMERA slowly PULLS BACK from the closeup we SEE that we have been looking into a mirror. She is standing before the full-length mirror in her bedroom doing her make-up. She overdoes it in the style of the time: rosebud mouth and so forth. As the film progresses her make-up will be refined until in the end, there is none.

The CAMERA PULLS BACK and continues to MOVE VERY SLOWLY throughout the first part of this scene. As the CAMERA continues to move away, we SEE, by degrees, that Bonnie is naked. Her nudity is never blatantly revealed to the audience, but implied. That is, she should be "covered" in various ways from the CAMERA'S P.O.V., but the audience must be aware of her exposure to Clyde later in the scene. This is the only time in the film that she will ever be this exposed, in all senses of the word, to the audience. Her attitude and appraisal of herself here are touched with narcissism.

The bedroom itself is a second-story bedroom in a lower-class frame house in West Dallas, Texas. The neighborhood is low income. Though the room reveals its shabby surroundings, it also reveals an attempt by Bonnie to fix it up. Small and corny *objets d'art* are all over the tops of the bureaus, vanity tables, etc. (Little glass figurines and porcelain statutettes and the like.)

Bonnie finishes admiring herself. She walks from the mirror and moves slowly across the room, the CAMERA moving with her, until she reaches the screened window on the opposite wall. The shade is up. There are no curtains. She looks out the window, looking down, and the CAMERA looks down with her.

2. *Ext. Bedroom   Bonnie's P.O.V.*   *Day*

Over her shoulder, we SEE the driveway leading to the garage connected to the house. There is an old car parked in the driveway, its windows open. We SEE a man walking up the driveway, somewhat furtively. He is a rather dapper fellow, dressed in a dark suit with a vest, a white collar, and a straw boater. It is CLYDE BARROW. Obviously, he is about to steal the car. He looks it over, checking around him to make sure no passers-by are coming. He peers inside the front window to see if the keys are in the ignition. He studies the dashboard. Bonnie continues watching, silently. Finally she calls out.

Bonnie: Hey, boy! What you doin' with my mama's car?

3. *Ext. Driveway*   *Day*

Clyde, startled, jumps and looks to see who has caught him. Obviously frightened, he looks up and his face freezes at what he sees.

4. *Ext. Window   Clyde's P.O.V.*   *Day*

We now SEE what he is looking at: at the open window, revealed from the waist up, is the naked Bonnie. She looks down, an impudent half-smile on her face. She doesn't move or make any attempt to cover herself.

5. *Ext. Closeup of Clyde*   *Day*

whose face changes from astonishment to an answering smile of impudence. (Seeing what he has, he realizes that this girl is clearly not going to scream for the police. Already they are in a little game instigated by Bonnie, sizing each other up, competing in a kind of playful arrogance. Before they speak, they have become co-conspirators.)

6. *Closeup of Bonnie*

still smiling. Finally she speaks:

Bonnie: Wait there!

7. *Int. Bedroom*   *Day*

Running from the window, she flings open a closet and grabs a dress, and shoes. She slips on the shoes, and flings the dress on, running out the door as she does. The CAMERA TRACKS with her, moving as fast. As she runs down the stairs she buttons up the dress.

8. *Ext. Driveway*   *Day*

She flies out the door, slamming it behind her, runs off the porch (all this has been one continuous movement since she left the window, in great haste) and continues quickly into the driveway. Four feet away from Clyde, she stops on a dime. They stand there, looking at each other, smiling the same challenge. For a few seconds, no one speaks, then:

Bonnie: (putting him on) Ain't you ashamed? Tryin' to steal an old lady's automobile.

Clyde: (with the same put-on) I been thinkin' about buyin' me one.

Bonnie: Bull. You ain't got money for dinner, let alone buy no car.

Clyde: (still the battle of wits going on) Now I got enough money for cokes, and since it don't look like you're gonna invite me inside—

Bonnie: You'd steal the dining room table if I did.

Clyde: (he moves from his spot) Come to town with me, then. How'd that be?

Bonnie: (starting to walk onto the sidewalk) Goin' to work anyway.

9. *Ext. Street*   *Moving Shot*   *Day*

The CAMERA TRACKS. It is a hot Texas afternoon, all white light and glare. As they walk the block to town in this scene, their manner of mutual impudence is still pervading.

Clyde: Goin' to work, huh? What do you do?

Bonnie: None of your business.

Clyde: (pretending to give it serious thought) I bet you're a . . . movie star! (thinks) No . . . A lady mechanic? . . . No . . . A maid?—

Bonnie: (really offended by that) What do you think I am?

Clyde: (right on the nose) A waitress.

Bonnie: (slightly startled by his accuracy, anxious to get back now that he is temporarily one-up) What line of work are you in? When you're not stealin' cars?

Clyde: (*mysteriously*) I tell you, I'm lookin' for suitable employment right at the moment.

Bonnie: What did you do before?

Clyde: (coolly knowing its effect) I was in State **Prison.**

Bonnie: State *Prison?* (she shows her surprise)

Clyde: Yeah.

Bonnie: (herself again) Guess *some* little old lady wasn't so nice.

Clyde: (tough) It was armed robbery.

Bonnie: (sarcastically) My, my, the things that turn up in the driveway these days.

They reach the corner and turn. They are on:

10. *Ext. Main Street*   *Day*

—a small-town street of barber shops, cafes, groceries, etc. At the moment, it is deserted. They continue walking down the empty street. Clyde looks the place over. TRACKING.

Clyde: What do y'all do for a good time around here, listen to the grass grow?

Bonnie: Guess you had a lot more fun up at State Prison, huh?

Clyde laughs, enjoying her repartee. They continue walking. At a hydrant, Clyde stops.

Clyde: (showing off, but seriously) See this foot? (pointing at his right foot) I chopped two toes off of it. With a axe.

Bonnie: (shocked) What? Why?

Clyde: To get off the damn work detail, that's why. (stopping) Want to see?

Bonnie: (a lady of some sensitivity) No! . . . (turning cute) I surely don't intend to stand here and look at your dirty feet in the middle of Main Street.

They continue walking in silence past a few stores, each planning what next to say.

Bonnie: Boy, did you really do that?

Clyde: Yeah.

Bonnie: You must be crazy.   DISSOLVE TO

11. *Ext. Gas Station*   *Day*

Gas station up the block. Bonnie and Clyde are seen leaning against the soft drink chest, their profiles silhouetted by the bright sun. They are drinking cokes. As they begin to talk, the CAMERA MOVES IN CLOSER to them. Clyde takes off his hat and rubs the cold coke bottle across his forehead. Bonnie watches him.

Bonnie: What's it like?

Clyde: Prison?

Bonnie: (very interested) No, armed robbery.

Clyde: (he thinks it a silly question) It's . . . I don't know . . . it isn't like anything.

Bonnie: (thinking she's heard proof that he's a liar) Hah! I knew you never robbed no place, you faker.

Clyde: (challenged) Oh, yeah? (studies her, then makes up his mind to show her)

12. *Closeup Gun*   Day

He reaches in his jacket and pulls out a gun. The CAMERA MOVES to a CLOSEUP of the gun, glinting in the sunlight.

13. *Ext. Street*   Day

The CAMERA PULLS BACK to SHOW Bonnie looking at it with fascination. The weapon has an immediate effect on her. She touches it in a manner almost sexual, full of repressed excitement.

Bonnie: (goading him on) Yeah, well you got one all right, I guess . . . but you wouldn't have the gumption to use it.

Clyde: (picking up the challenge, proving himself) You just keep your eyes open.

14. *Ext. Little Grocery Store Across the Street*   Day

The CAMERA remains just behind Bonnie's shoulder so that throughout the following scene we have Bonnie in the picture, looking at what we look at.

Clyde goes into the little store. We remain outside with Bonnie watching. For a minute nothing happens. We can barely see what is going on in the store. Then Clyde comes out, walking slowly. In one hand he holds the gun, in the other a fistful of money. He gets halfway to Bonnie and smiles broadly at her, a smile of charm and personality. She smiles back. The moment is intense, as if a spark has jumped from one to the other. Their relationship, which began the minute Bonnie spotted him in the driveway, has now really begun. Clyde has shown his stuff and Bonnie is "turned on."

Suddenly the old man who runs the grocery store comes running out into the street, completely dumbfounded. He stands there and says nothing, yet his mouth moves in silent protest. Clyde points the gun above him and fires. It is the first loud noise in the film thus far and it should be a shock. The old man, terrified, runs back into the store as fast as he can. Clyde quickly grabs Bonnie's hand. The CAMERA SWINGS with them as they turn and begin to run down the street. A few yards and the stores disappear entirely. The landscape turns into that arid, flat and unrelieved western plain that begins where the town ends.

15. *Ext. Store At the Edge of Town*   *Day*

A car is parked at the back of the store. As soon as they reach it, Clyde motions and Bonnie gets in. Clyde runs to the front, lifts up the hood and crosses the wires to make it start. As he stands back, Bonnie calls to him:

Bonnie: Hey, what's your name, anyway?

Clyde: (he slams the hood) Clyde Barrow.

He runs over to the door, opens it, shoves her over, and starts up the engine. The entire sequence is played at an incredibly rapid pace.

Bonnie: (loud, to make herself heard over the gunning motor) Hi, I'm Bonnie Parker. Please to meet you.

16. *Ext. Road*   *Day*

VROOM! The car zooms off down the road, doing 90. The fast country breakdown MUSIC starts up on the sound track, going just as fast as the car.

II. THE GUN BATTLE AT JOPLIN (FINAL-SCRIPT VERSION)

Clyde: (seeing it) It's the law.

(*Note:*   The three major gun battles in this film of which this is the first, each have a different emotional and cinematic quality. The quality for this Joplin debacle is chaos, hysteria, extremely rapid movement and lots of noise. The audience should be assaulted. From the moment Clyde cries out, and throughout all the following action, Blanche, in blind panic, SCREAMS hysterically. The scream persists through the gunfire, never lessening on the soundtrack. Its effects should be at first funny to the audience, then annoying, and finally terrifying.

As soon as Clyde calls out, Blanche drops the frying pan on the floor and begins SCREAMING. CAMERA CUTS BACK to the living room. Everyone else leaps into action. Guns begin blazing from everywhere; we rarely see who is shooting at whom.)

101. *Ext. Garage Apartment*   *Day*

The police, we see in OUTSIDE SHOT, are lined up in the street, firing. There are about ten of them.

102. *Int. Garage Apartment* *Day*

The gang runs down the stairs into the garage—we follow them with a hand-held CAMERA TRACKING rapidly.

103. *Ext. Street* *Day*

Blanche, however, in utter panic, just runs right out the front door, and begins running down the quiet residential street, going nowhere, anywhere.

104. *Ext. Garage Apartment* *Day*

Buck, crouching, shooting with one hand, gets the garage door open. A policeman FIRES. Buck FIRES back and the cop falls dead in the street. Buck, FIRING, dashes to the police car blocking their escape and releases the hand brake. Clyde, Bonnie and C. W. leap into their car, gun the motor, still shooting madly. Two more police fall dead or wounded. One policeman is hurled through a fence by the blast of a sawed-off shotgun. Buck jumps into the car with the others. They now begin to bump the police car with their car. The police car picks up speed as they push it and it tears into the street right at the group of firing police. The gang's car turns into the street in a hail of bullets and takes off down the street toward the running Blanche. Bonnie and Clyde are in front; Buck and C. W. in the back seat firing back at police. The car pulls alongside the wildly running Blanche; the back door is flung open and in almost the style of a cartoon, two hands reach out and lift her off her feet and pull her into the car. They speed away.

CUT TO:

105. *Int. Car* *Day*

The inside of the car, still speeding. Blanche is hysterical. C. W. is still FIRING out the window. The pursuing police car's driver is shot and the car CRASHES into a tree. The gang is not being pursued now, but Clyde is driving at 90. Blanche is MOANING and CRYING. Bonnie, in front, turns around furiously.

Bonnie: Dammit, you almost got us killed!

Blanche: (crying) What did I do wrong? I s'pose you'd be happier if I got shot.

Bonnie: (at her bitchiest) Yeah, it would of saved us all a lot of trouble.

Blanche: Buck, don't let that woman talk to me like that!

Buck: (caught in the middle of a bad situation, knowing Blanche is wrong, but trying to soothe her) You shouldn't have done it, Blanche.

III. FINAL-SCRIPT VERSION OF POEM-READING SCENE

FADE IN:

232. *Ext. Car on the Jones Farm   A Dirt Path Near the Barn   Day*

It is pouring rain, middle of the afternoon, Bonnie and Clyde are inside the car, sitting. They have lived so much in cars that they tend to still spend much of their time in it rather than in a room. There they are themselves.

233. *Int. Car*

Bonnie is in the back seat, her legs wrapped in a plaid blanket, writing poetry. She looks like Elizabeth Barrett Browning. With one essential difference—her arm is in a sling and she is wearing bandages on the shoulder. Clyde is in the front seat, reading a newspaper. He is also partially bandaged. On the dashboard is a box of ginger-snaps which he eats while he reads. They look domestic.

Clyde: Want a ginger-snap, Bonnie?

Bonnie: (busy, absorbed) No, hum-umm. (then she realizes his nice gesture and smiles warmly at him) But thanks anyway, Clyde. (She takes it all in, her situation, and looks content and cozy) It's real nice here, just the two of us like this.

Clyde: (more interested in his paper) Uh-huh. (something in the paper catches his interest) Look here, honey, remember this?

He holds up the paper; there is one of the photos from the motel, the one showing Bonnie smoking. She looks up at it with mild interest.

Bonnie: Yeah, at the motel.

Clyde: (studying the picture) You sure don't resemble that no more.

234. *Closeup Bonnie*

She doesn't. She has become totally fragile, the essence of herself. She is writing on a pad.

235. *Clyde and Bonnie*

Clyde: What you writin' this time?

Bonnie: I'm writing a poem about us. I'm writing *our* story.

Clyde: (this appeals to his ego) Oh, are you? Let's hear it. If it's good, I'll mail it into the Law and it'll be printed in all the papers again.

Bonnie: Just let me finish this line.

She does so. Clyde munches a cookie.

Bonnie: (continuing) Okay, here it is.

236. *Closeup Bonnie*

as she reads intensely. At the beginning of this montage, the CAMERA
REMAINS on her face. Behind her we SEE the rain on the window.

Bonnie: (reading)

"The Story of Bonnie and Clyde"
You've heard the story of Jesse James—
Of how he lived and died:
   If you're still in need
   Of something to read
Here's the story of Bonnie and Clyde.

Now Bonnie and Clyde are the Barrow Gang
I'm sure you all have read
   How they rob and steal
   And those who squeal
Are usually found dying or dead.

They call them cold-hearted killers;
They say they are heartless and mean;
   But I say this with pride,
   That I once knew Clyde
When he was honest and upright and clean.

But the laws fooled around,
   Kept taking him down
   And locking him up in a cell,
Till he said to me,
   "I'll never be free
So I'll meet a few of them in hell."

The road was so dimly lighted;
There were no highway signs to guide;
   But they made up their minds
   If all roads were blind,
They wouldn't give up till they died.

CUT TO:

237. *Int. Police Station*   *Day*

The manuscript is lying on the police blotter. Hamer picks it up and
continues reading it. He reads it in a halting way.

Hamer:

The road gets dimmer and dimmer;
Sometimes you can hardly see;
   But it's fight man to man,
   And do all you can,
For they know they can never be free.

> From heartbreak some people have suffered;
> From weariness some people have died;
>   But take it all in all,
>   Our troubles are small,
> Till we get like Bonnie and Clyde.

238. *Closeup of a Newspaper Page*

The poem is printed all the way down the length of one column. On the sound track, Bonnie's VOICE picks up the recitation:

> *Bonnie's Voice:* (O.S.)
> If a policeman is killed in Dallas,
> And they have no clue or guide;
>   If they can't find a fiend,
>   They just wipe their slate clean
> And hang it on Bonnie and Clyde.

239. *Int. Car Closeup of Bonnie*   *Day*

The day is sunny as we see it through the car window. She continues reading, but now she reads it directly from the newspaper:

> *Bonnie:*
> If they try to act like citizens
> And rent them a nice little flat
>   About the third night
>   They're invited to fight
> By a sub-gun's rat-tat-tat.

> Some day they'll go down together;
> They'll bury them side by side;
>   To few it'll be grief—
>   To the law a relief—
> But it's death for Bonnie and Clyde.

Bonnie finishes the poem, as CAMERA PULLS BACK SLIGHTLY to show that it is a different day, different clothes and the bandages are gone. As she stops, she has an expectant and somewhat self-satisfied look.

240. *Closeup of Clyde*

His eyes are wide, his mouth open, his face shows surprise and delight and he is on the verge of a giant laugh.

Clyde: (in gleeful wonder) *Damn!* That's me!

A great laugh comes bursting from him. CAMERA WIDENS to take in Bonnie. She is both startled and delighted by his response.

Clyde: (continuing) In that poem!

Bonnie giggles.

Clyde: (continuing; it is all starting to come out now—his realization that he has made it, that he is the stuff of legend, that he is an important figure) A sub-gun's rat-tat-tat! (he begins to lough loudly) Right in the paper!

241. *Closeup Bonnie*

Now laughing too, with a great feeling of joy.

242. *Two Shot Bonnie and Clyde*

Clyde: Jesse James! You hear 'bout old Jesse, now you goin' to hear 'bout Clyde! He puffs up with air and explodes like a steam valve.

Clyde: (continuing) *Pshhhhhh!*

He grabs Bonnie and chuckles delightedly.

Clyde: (continuing) Damn, Bonnie! You musta been one hell of a waitress!

243. *Closeup Bonnie*

Laughing, her eyes filled with tears. Clyde's hand wipes them away.

244. *Two Shot*

Clyde: (shaking his head back and forth like a puppy, just so much glee in him that he can't hold it) Oooooh, that Clyde! That's my boy, that Clyde!

He looks at her with love and delight, hugs her tightly.

Clyde: Bonnie . . . (she hugs him back) The Poem of Bonnie and Clyde!

Bonnie: (laughing at the mistake, happy) The *Story.*

Clyde: The *Story* of Bonnie and Clyde! Oh, child, you really did tell that story!

He pulls her to him, his face inches away from hers, about to kiss her. She is waiting, expecting. . . . Suddenly, he lets out one wild laugh almost into her mouth.

He kisses her. She kisses back. They are chuckling, giggling. They grow more ardent; they pull back and laugh again. They begin to make love.

IV. ORIGINAL-SCRIPT VERSION OF POEM-READING SCENE

FADE IN:

104. *Ext. Car—Day*

Exterior of the Jones farm, a dirt path near the barn. It is pouring rain, middle of the afternoon. Bonnie and Clyde are inside the car, sitting.

They have lived so much in cars that they tend to still spend much of their time in it rather than in a room. There they are themselves.

Interior of the car. Bonnie is in the back seat, her legs wrapped in a plaid blanket, writing poetry. She looks like Elizabeth Barrett Browning. Clyde is in the front seat reading a newspaper. On the dashboard is a box of ginger-snaps which he eats while he reads. They look domestic.

Clyde: Want a ginger-snap, Bonnie?

Bonnie: (busy, absorbed) No, hum-umm.

Clyde goes back to his paper, gets engrossed in something.

Clyde: Look here, honey, remember this?

He holds up the paper; there is one of the photos from the motel, the one showing Bonnie smoking. She looks up at it with mild interest.

Bonnie: Yeah, at the motel.

Clyde: (studying the picture) You sure don't resemble that no more.

She doesn't. She has become totally fragile, the essence of herself. Close-up Bonnie, writing on a pad.

Clyde: What you writin' this time?

Bonnie: (intensely) I'm writing a poem about us. I'm writing *our* story.

Clyde: (this appeals to his ego) Oh, are you? Let's hear it. If it's good, I'll mail it into the law and it'll be printed in all the papers again.

Bonnie: Just let me finish this line.

She does so. Clyde munches a cookie.

Bonnie: Okay, here it is.

Close-up Bonnie as she reads intensely. At the beginning of this montage, the camera remains on her face. Behind her we see the rain on the window.

Bonnie: (reading)

> "The Story of Bonnie and Clyde"
> You've heard the story of Jesse James—
> Of how he lived and died;
> > If you're still in need
> > Of something to read
> Here's the story of Bonnie and Clyde.
>
> Now Bonnie and Clyde are the Barrow gang.
> I'm sure you all have read
> > How they rob and steal
> > And those who squeal
> Are usually found dying or dead.
>
> They call them cold-hearted killers;
> They say they are heartless and mean;

> But I say this with pride,
> That I once knew Clyde
> When he was honest and upright and clean.

> But the laws fooled around,
> Kept taking him down
> And locking him up in a cell,
> Till he said to me,
> "I'll never be free
> So I'll meet a few of them in hell."

> The road was so dimly lighted;
> There were no highway signs to guide;
> But they made up their minds
> If all roads were blind,
> They wouldn't give up till they died.

105. *Int. Police Station—Day*

Cut to a police station. The manuscript is lying on the police blotter. A policeman picks it up and continues reading it. He reads it very badly, in a halting, stammering way.

> *Policeman:*
> The road gets dimmer and dimmer;
> Sometimes you can hardly see;
> But it's fight, man to man,
> And do all you can,
> For they know they can never be free.

> From heart-break some people have suffered;
> From weariness some people have died;
> But take it all in all,
> Our troubles are small
> Till we get like Bonnie and Clyde.

Cut to close-up of a newspaper page. The poem is printed all the way down the length of one column. On the soundtrack, Bonnie's voice picks up the recitation.

> *Bonnie:*
> If a policeman is killed in Dallas,
> And they have no clue or guide;
> If they can't find a fiend,
> They just wipe their slate clean
> And hang it on Bonnie and Clyde.

106. *Ext. Car—Day*

Cut to close-up of Bonnie again, still in the car, but it is another day, and she is wearing different clothing. The day is sunny as we see it through the car window. She continues reading, but now she reads it directly from the newspaper.

Bonnie:
If they try to act like citizens
And rent them a nice little flat
   About the third night
   They're invited to fight
By a sub-gun's rat-tat-tat.

Some day they'll go down together;
They'll bury them side by side;
   To few it'll be grief—
   To the law a relief—
But it's death for Bonnie and Clyde.

Bonnie finishes the poem with a look of great satisfaction. CAMERA pulls back again to reveal Clyde in the car with her, as before, except dressed in different clothes. Clyde is staring out the front window, moody, hardly listening to what she has been reading.

Clyde is staring out the windshield, abstractedly performing his flashy gun spin over and over and over.

Bonnie: (with an artist's pride) I think that's better'n all my other poetry, don't you, Clyde?

Clyde: (abstractly, distracted) Yeah, honey, fine.

Bonnie: (she wanted a bigger response) Well what do you mean "Yeah honey, fine." Don't you think it's my best piece of poetry?

Clyde: Uh-huh.

A pause. Clyde continues twirling his gun.

Bonnie: (changing subject, looking cozily content) This is nice, ain't it? Just the two of us like this.

Clyde: (his mind far away, talking half to himself) Wished Buck was here . . .

Bonnie: Buck. If it wasn't him it'd be somebody else. (deadly serious) That's the truth, ain't it, Clyde.

Clyde: (admitting it at last) Yeah, that's the truth.

There is tense silence now; an understanding has been reached. But it is all uncomfortable and Clyde has to squirm out of it. He feels guilty, tries to rationalize.

Well . . . ain't nothin' wrong with my missin' Buck. He's my family.

Bonnie: I'm your family, too.

Shot favors Clyde, showing his expression as he realizes the great truth of what she's said. Bonnie, mad, gets out of the car, slamming the door. We go out with her.

She walks towards the front of the car and a bit past it. She looks back, sees Clyde still sitting behind the wheel, twirling his gun.

She very deliberately takes out her gun and suddenly jumps up on the hood of the car, peering into the windshield so that only an inch of glass separates them. She points her gun directly at Clyde through the window, startling him, and then begins twirling it in perfect synchronization with his.

Clyde begins to laugh, though we hear the sound muffled inside the car and see his face through the sunlight glinting off the windshield. As Clyde laughs and continues spinning the gun, Bonnie slowly starts to smile.

Filmography[1]

COMPLETED FILMS

The Left-handed Gun, Warner Brothers. 1957.
The Miracle Worker, United Artists. 1962.
Mickey One, Columbia. 1964.
The Chase, Columbia. 1965.
Bonnie and Clyde, Warner Brothers. 1967.
Alice's Restaurant, United Artists. 1969.
Little Big Man, Cinema Center. 1970.

TELEVISION DIRECTION

First Person, NBC. 1953.
Philco Playhouse, NBC. 1953–55.
The Miracle Worker, Portrait of a Murderer, Private Property.
  1956.
Charley's Aunt, Playhouse 90. 1958.
Flesh and Blood, NBC. 1967.

THEATRICAL DIRECTION

Blue Denim, 1954.
Two for the Seesaw, by William Gibson. 1957–58.
The Miracle Worker, by William Gibson. 1959.
Toys in the Attic, by Lillian Hellman. 1960.
An Evening with Nichols and May, 1960.
All the Way Home, by Tad Mosel. 1960.
In the Counting House, by Leslie Wiener, 1962.

[1] For more complete lists of casts and credits see the filmography in Robin Wood, *Arthur Penn* (New York: Frederick A. Praeger, Inc., 1970).

Lorenzo, by Jack Richardson. 1963.
Golden Boy, with Sammy Davis Jr. 1964.
Wait Until Dark, by Frederick Knott. 1966.

DOCUMENTARY

Arthur Penn: Themes and Variants. 1970. A documentary on Arthur Penn and his work, directed, written, and produced by Robert P. S. B. Hughes.

Selected Bibliography

I. THE CRIMINAL IN DRAMA AND FILM; THE GANGSTER FILM

Altick, Richard D. *Victorian Studies in Scarlet,* pp. 41–114. New York: W. W. Norton & Company, 1970. Fascinating account of the literary and theatrical treatment of crime in the Victorian age, the artistic background of the contemporary crime film.

Baxter, John. *The Gangster Film.* New York, A. S. Barnes & Co., Inc., 1970. Alphabetically arranged reference book listing major directors, actors, and writers of gangster films. Also includes an alphabetical index of over 1000 gangster films.

Karpf, Stephen L. *The Gangster Film: Emergence, Variation and Decay of a Genre, 1930–1940.* Unpublished Ph.D. dissertation, Northwestern University, August, 1969.

Warshow, Robert. "The Gangster as Tragic Hero." *The Immediate Experience.* Garden City, N.Y.: Doubleday & Company, Inc., 1962. The classic essay on the gangster film.

Wilkinson, George Theodore. "Richard Ferguson (Galloping Dick): Convicted at the Lent Assizes, 1800, at Aylesburn, and Executed for a Highway Robbery." *The Newgate Calendar.* London: Panther Books, 1962. An early nineteenth-century account of a bandit, the pattern of whose fate bears considerable resemblance to that of the gangster in the modern gangster film.

II. THE HISTORICAL BONNIE AND CLYDE: VARIOUS ACCOUNTS

* "Barrow and Woman Are Slain by Police in Louisiana Trap," "Officers Picture Barrow Slaying," "Barrow's Killings Date from Parole." *The New York Times* (May 24, 1934).

* Fortune, Jan I., ed. *The True Story of Bonnie and Clyde: As Told*

* An asterisk denotes a selection reprinted in this volume.

by Bonnie's Mother and Clyde's Sister. New York, N.Y.: Signet Books, 1968. A sympathetic account of Bonnie and Clyde, obviously biased, but moving and colorful. An important source for many of the central episodes in the film. Originally published as *Fugitives* (Dallas, Texas: The Ranger Press, 1934).

Jenkins, John H., and Gordon Frost. *I'm Frank Hamer: The Life of a Texas Peace Officer.* Austin, Texas and New York, N.Y.: The Pemberton Press, 1968. Biography of the man who tracked down Bonnie and Clyde. Much information on the pair from Hamer's point of view.

Portley, Edward, with C. F. Waers. "Killer Gang." *Master Detective* (February, 1945): 36–84. A long and detailed account of the Barrow gang by the former chief of detectives of Joplin, Missouri.

Rogers, John William. *The Lusty Texans of Dallas.* Dallas, Texas: The Cokesbury Bookstore, 1965. Not too much information on Bonnie and Clyde, but a very interesting account of the social and cultural background of Dallas, the home of the two outlaws.

Toland, John. *The Dillinger Days.* New York, N.Y.: Random House, 1963. Journalistic but solid account of the gangs of the early thirties, including the Barrow gang.

* Webb, Walter Prescott. *The Texas Rangers.* Austin, Texas: University of Texas Press, 1965 (Originally published, 1935). Includes Frank Hamer's account of his killing of Bonnie and Clyde.

III. Arthur Penn: General Studies and Personal Statements

Gelmis, Joseph. *The Film Director as Superstar.* Garden City, N.Y.: Doubleday & Company, Inc. 1970. Interviews with several directors, including Arthur Penn.

* Hillier, Jim. "Arthur Penn." *Screen* 10, no. 1 (January/February 1969): 5–13.

Penn, Arthur. "*Bonnie and Clyde:* Private Morality and Public Violence." *Take One* 1, no. 6: 20–22.

* Penn, Arthur, with Jean-Louis Comolli, and Andre S. Labarthe. "*Bonnie and Clyde:* An Interview with Arthur Penn." *Evergreen Review* 12, no. 55 (June 1968): 61–63. Translated and reprinted from *Cahiers du Cinéma.*

Rubin, Martin, and Eric Sherman. *The Director's Event.* New York,

N.Y.: Atheneum Publishers, 1970. An interview mainly concerned with *Bonnie and Clyde*. Very useful as a statement of Penn's interpretation of the film.

Wood, Robin. *Arthur Penn*. New York, N.Y.: Frederick A. Praeger, Inc., 1970. Excellent critical study of the films of Arthur Penn. Has a good chapter on Bonnie and Clyde, as well as complete filmography.

IV. ESSAYS AND REVIEWS ON *Bonnie and Clyde*

Armstrong, Marion. "Study in Infantilism." *Christian Century* 84 (October 18, 1967): 1326.

Chevallier, Jacques. *"Bonnie et Clyde." Image et Son* 216 (April 1968): 106–8.

* Collier, Peter. "The Barrow Gang: An Aftertaste." *Ramparts* 6 (May 1968): 16–22.

Conroy, Frank. "Violent Movies." *The New York Review of Books* 11, no. 1 (July 11, 1968): 28–29.

* Cook, Page, *"Bonnie and Clyde." Films in Review* 18, no. 8 (October 1967): 504–5.

Crist, Judith. *"Bonnie and Clyde,* 'Triumph.' " *Vogue* 150 (September 15, 1967): 68.

* Crowther, Bosley, *"Bonnie and Clyde." The New York Times* (August 14, 1967).

Farber, Stephen. *"Bonnie and Clyde." Sight and Sound 37,* no. 4 (Autumn 1968): 174–75.

* Free, William J. "Aesthetic and Moral Value in *Bonnie and Clyde."* Quarterly Journal of Speech 54 (October 1968): 220–25.

* Geduld, Carolyn. *"Bonnie and Clyde*: Society Vs. the Clan." *Film Heritage* 3, no. 2 (Winter 1967–68). Reprinted in Julius Bellone, ed., *Renaissance of the Film*. New York, N.Y.: The Crowell-Collier Publishing Co., 1970.

Gilman, Richard. "Gangsters on the Road to Nowhere." *New Republic* 157 (November 4, 1967): 27–29.

Harcourt, Peter. "In Defense of Film History." In *Perspectives on the Study of Film,* edited by John Stuart Katz. Boston, Mass.: Little, Brown and Company, 1971. Brief but perceptive analysis of *Bonnie and Clyde* is a part of this essay.

Jacobs, Jay, "Bloody Murder." *The Reporter* 37 (October 5, 1967): 46–47.

*Johnson, Albert. *"Bonnie and Clyde." Film Quarterly* 21, no. 2 (Winter 1967–68): 45–48.

Kael, Pauline. *"Bonnie and Clyde." The New Yorker* 43 (October 21, 1967): 141–71. A brilliant discussion of the film not included in this anthology only because of its ready availability elsewhere, e.g., in *Kiss Kiss Bang Bang,* Boston, Little, Brown and Company, 1968; or in *Film 67/68,* New York, N.Y.: Simon and Schuster, Inc., 1968.

Kauffman, Stanley, *"Bonnie and Clyde." New American Review,* no. 2 (January 1968). Reprinted with a postscript in Kauffman's *Figures of Light* (New York, Harper and Row, 1971).

Laura, Ernesto G. *"Bonnie and Clyde." Bianco e Nero* 29, nos. 3–4 (March–April 1968): 153–56.

* Lawson, John Howard. "Our Film and Theirs: *Grapes of Wrath* and *Bonnie and Clyde."* American Dialog 5 (Winter 1968–69): 30–33.

Milne, Tom. *"Bonnie and Clyde." Sight and Sound* 36, no. 4 (Autumn 1967): 203–4.

Quirk, John. "Violent Romanticism." Commonweal 87 (November 10, 1967): 170–71.

Richard, Jerry. "Foggy Bottom." *The Antioch Review* 28, no. 3: 388–92.

* Samuels, Charles T. "The American Scene: *Bonnie and Clyde." Hudson Review* 21 (Spring 1968): 10–22.

Schickel, Richard and John Simon, eds. *Film 67/68.* New York, N.Y. Simon and Schuster, Inc., 1968. Includes essays on *Bonnie and Clyde* by Joseph Morgenstern, John Simon, Stanley Kauffman, and Pauline Kael.

* Schickel, Richard. "Flaws in a Savage Satire." *Life* 63 (October 13, 1967): 16.

Sheed, Wilfrid. "Films." *Esquire* 68 (November and December 1967). Sheed's November column is a review of *Bonnie and Clyde.* The December column is an interesting essay on the representation of violence in films with a few comments on *Bonnie and Clyde.*

* Steele, Robert. "The Good-bad and the Bad-good in Movies: *Bonnie and Clyde* and *In Cold Blood."* The Catholic World 207 (May 1968): 76–79.

Time. "Low-down Hoedown." Vol. 90 (August 25, 1967): 78. "The Shock of Freedom in Films." Vol. 90 (December 8, 1978): 66. The first selection is a brief, negative review. The second, a full-scale cover essay on *Bonnie and Clyde* and the new trends in film it represents.

Towne, Robert, "A Trip with Bonnie and Clyde." *Cinema* 3, no. 5 (Summer 1967): 4–7.

Walsh, Moira. *"Bonnie and Clyde." America* 117 (September 2, 1967): 227.

Index